ACRL Publications in Librarianship no. 40

Book Selling and Book Buying

Aspects of the Nineteenth-Century British and North American Book Trade

Edited by

RICHARD G. LANDON

American Library Association

Chicago 1978

Library of Congress Cataloging in Publication Data

Main entry under title:

Book selling and book buying.

(ACRL publications in librarianship ; no. 40)
Papers presented at a conference of the Rare Books
and Manuscripts Section held in Toronto, June 14-17,
1977.

1. Book industries and trade—Great Britain—
History—19th century—Congresses. 2. Book industries
and trade—North America—History—19th century—
Congresses. 3. Book collecting—History—19th century
—Congresses. I. Landon, Richard G. II. Association
of College and Research Libraries. Rare Books and
Manuscripts Section. III. Title. IV. Series:
Association of College and Research Libraries. ACRL
publications in librarianship ; no. 40.

Z674.A75 no. 40 [Z325] 658.8'09'0705730941 78-31812
ISBN 0-8389-3224-X

Contents

Preface

This volume makes available in permanent form the papers presented at the conference of the Rare Books and Manuscripts Section held in Toronto, June 14-17, 1977. This was the Section's 18th conference in a series launched in 1959 and continuing unbroken with the exception of 1960, when no meeting was held. The conferences are traditionally held in the days immediately preceding the annual conference of the American Library Association.

At the Section's first two conferences the programs featured panel discussions on topics of interest to rare book librarians, antiquarian book dealers, bibliographers, and collectors. Although the intended audience has remained the same over the years, the programs have increasingly featured scholarly papers organized around a single large theme. At the 3rd conference in 1962, for which Frances J. Brewer served as the Section Chairperson, the theme was Book Illustration. The papers presented at the conference, as edited by Mrs. Brewer, were published by Gebr. Mann Verlag in Berlin in 1963. The proceedings of the 4th conference (1964) on Bibliography and Natural History were edited by Thomas R. Buckman and published by the University of Kansas Libraries in 1966. The theme of the 1975 conference, held in San Francisco, was Eighteenth-Century Books Considered by Librarians and Booksellers, Bibliographers, Collectors. The proceedings, edited by the Section Chairperson,

Hendrik Edelman, were printed by Cornell University in 1976 and made available through the Association of College and Research Libraries (ACRL) in Chicago. The proceedings of the 1976 Ann Arbor Conference on Maps and Atlases have been published by the *AB Bookman's Yearbook*.

This brief summary of some of the highlights of the Section's history can be amplified by consulting Robert J. Adelsperger's 1974 paper, "Outline History of ACRL Rare Book and Manuscript Section," copies of which can be obtained from the Secretary of the Section. The paper prepared and distributed by Georgia C. Haugh at the 1976 conference in Ann Arbor, "A Brief Review of the Committee on Rare Books and Events Leading to the Rare Books Section of ACRL, 1955-1958," discusses the Section's entire history.

The executive secretaries of ACRL have played a large part in the success of the conferences, and I particularly wish to express my gratitude to Beverly Lynch, the incumbent in that office during most of my term as Section Chairperson. Dr. Lynch encouraged me to propose to the ACRL Editorial Board that the proceedings of the Toronto conference be published as an ACRL monograph. The gratifying results of that suggestion are now before you. This is the first time ACRL has officially sponsored the publication of the proceedings of a Section conference. The appropriateness of such an action is, I hope, clear from my summary history of the Section.

As the title of this volume makes evident, the theme of the 1977 conference was Book Selling and Book Buying: Aspects of Nineteenth-Century British and American Book Trades. The attendance was one of the largest ever, a tribute to the attractions of Toronto (this was the first time the Section had met in Canada) and to the hard work of the program and local arrangements committees, chaired by Richard G. Landon and Alan J. Horne, respectively. The exhibits mounted at the University of Toronto in the Thomas Fisher Rare Book Library, Massey College, and the E. J. Pratt Library of Victoria University, plus those at the Osborne Collection of the Toronto Public Libraries, underlined the appropriateness of holding a meeting in Toronto on nineteenth-century British and American book trades. It is a pleasure to extend my thanks to Mr. Landon, Mr. Horne, and their fellow committee members; to the host institution, the University of Toronto and the Chief Librarian Robert Blackburn; to the Toronto antiquarian book dealers; and to all the institutions and individuals who contributed to making the conference both a scholarly success and a warm and personal experience for all the attendees.

WILLIAM MATHESON
Chief of the Rare Books and
  Special Collections Division
Library of Congress

Introduction

Richard G. Landon

Richard G. Landon is the Head of the Thomas Fisher Rare Book Library, University of Toronto.

"Book selling and book buying: aspects of nineteenth-century British and North American book trades" is the rather imposing title chosen for the 18th annual ACRL Rare Books and Manuscripts Preconference. The theme suggests the two general aspects of the book trade which are of greatest concern to special collections librarians, collectors, and antiquarian booksellers. Toronto was a particularly appropriate city in which to hold the conference since the city's early history is also nineteenth-century and the development of its publishing and bookselling industries was largely a result of nineteenth-century development of those trades in Great Britain and the United States. The word "aspects" in the conference title was chosen deliberately, for it was of course impossible to cover completely the book trades that produced for a century profound revolutions in the manufacture and distribution of books. Indeed each of the papers presented dealt with a specific "aspect" which illustrated and illuminated the overall changes.

Book historians would generally agree that much work remains to be done on the nineteenth century and that it is only in comparatively recent times that serious attention has been paid to the complexities of nineteenth-century publishing and bookselling. This conference and this volume of papers, then, can be viewed as a contribution to a greater understanding of a neglected area of study of direct and serious interest to an increasing number of historians as well as the conference delegates. For-

1

mal discussion of the papers at the meetings was limited, but there was a great deal of informal exchange of information among the conference members.

The general theme of the conference was approached and examined differently by each of the speakers but two major areas emerged: publishing and collecting. The first five papers presented aspects of nineteenth-century book trades essentially concerned with the production and distribution of books. Two papers examined the traditions of collecting—one for the late nineteenth century itself and the other, modern collecting of nineteenth-century books. New information and fresh perceptions were presented by each speaker concerning his or her specific aspect and all contributed to an increased overall understanding of this complex but fascinating subject.

Terry Belanger's paper provides a kind of introduction to the conference theme. He discusses eighteenth-century bookselling to demonstrate its influence on the development of the great nineteenth-century publishing firms of London. He further suggests that the beginnings of many of the great Victorian publishing firms were based on antiquarian bookselling. The reasons for the disintegration of the close business relationship, perhaps best epitomized by the "conger," or loose trade association among members of the London book trade in the late eighteenth century, are complex, but from this breakdown emerges nineteenth-century publishing. Belanger's paper moves from the eighteenth-century world of Thomas Longman I to the Victorian world of Daniel Macmillan and sets the stage for an examination of more specialized facets of that later milieu.

To Judith St. John, "Victoria's day" means the first forty-two years, 1819-61, of the Queen's long life. During that period the publishers of children's books emerge as important specialist firms which take advantage of the burgeoning of popular culture and, in their turn, exert a profound effect on the quality of the literature produced for children. St. John points out that "the publishers and booksellers of the nineteenth-century were . . . the ultimate censors of the world of books" because they accepted or rejected manuscripts, encouraged or discouraged writers, and decided what books remained in print. This definition is made possible by the emergence of publishers as a distinct entity—the entrepreneurs of the book world. John Harris, along with many of his colleagues in the trade, brought about an important change in children's literature: the moral, often gloomy, tales of the eighteenth century giving way to books like *The Butterfly's Ball*. The publishers of children's books during "Victoria's day" laid the foundations of the booming trade in the marvelously illustrated children's books of the latter half of the nineteenth century. Their contribution, as set forth by St. John, is indeed one of the most fascinating aspects of the nineteenth-century book trades.

A very different, but equally fascinating, publishing activity of the nineteenth century is covered by Mihai Handrea. The publication of books in parts, a phenomenon which reached its peak in the nineteenth century, is most often considered in connection with the works of such popular novelists as Charles Dickens. Handrea, however, discusses books ranging from Hannah Maria Jones's *The Victim of Fashion* to the *Original Works of Hogarth* and has chosen as a particular example the publisher Thomas Kelly and his sensationally successful *An Authentic and Faithful History of the Mysterious Murder of Maria Marten in the Red Barn*. This is publishing at its nineteenth-century lurid best. Equally interesting, however, is Handrea's discussion of the distribution techniques of the publishers of part books and the development of the "canvasser." Thus another little known aspect of nineteenth-century publishing has been elucidated and described.

Still another neglected facet of the nineteenth-century book trade is the syndication of fiction. The conference was fortunate to have as a speaker Michael Turner, whose work on Tillotson's "Fiction Bureau" is well known. Tillotson was the largest and most enterprising of the provincial newspaper bureaus, applying to fiction the syndication techniques commonly used for news and advertisements. The agreements entered into between the Bureau and the many popular authors whose work appeared in this serialized form were complex, particularly regarding rights, and thus Tillotson was directly involved in the division of literary property into different kinds of publishing rights. Fiction in newspapers, which has obvious bibliographical and textual implications, was originally justified in a straightforward manner: it raised the rank of the paper and increased circulation. At the same time, as Turner concludes, it introduced "the masses of the lower working classes to fiction of a somewhat higher order than they had previously been used to." Tillotson's "obscure by-way of Victorian publishing history" is an aspect of nineteenth-century book trades with profound effects.

In the true spirit of cultural nationalism the Programme Committee felt that some "Canadian content" would be desirable. Thus Douglas Lochhead examines in some detail the activities of a nineteenth-century Toronto publisher, John Ross Robertson. The foundation of this study "had its beginnings as a venture in nineteenth-century Canadian historical bibliography," and the gaps in our knowledge of this general subject are very wide indeed. Lochhead's paper on Robertson focuses on his paper-back series (including some pirated titles) and much of Lochhead's information is gleaned from book advertisements contained in the *Toronto Evening Telegram*. Indeed, an analysis of publishing became, in many ways, an analysis of book promotion. A generality touched upon by other conference papers is again emphasized: Robertson's peculiar form of publishing was a response to a general public demand, felt strongly in Canada as well as in Great Britain and the United States, for cheap books.

With the paper of Franklin Gilliam a new focus on the aspects of nineteenth-century book selling and book buying asserts itself. Almost every conference delegate had an immediate and practical concern with the collecting, preservation, and availability of nineteenth-century books for research purposes. That the books were produced in enormous numbers in a bewildering variety of formats was made abundantly clear by several of the speakers. Where are those books now? The sobering theme of Gilliam's paper, supported by an array of statistics, is that for many authors deemed worthy of historical and critical consideration there are no adequate collections available nor are there ever likely to be. When a distinguished collection, such as that of the University of California at Los Angeles, can muster only a small percentage of the titles of an author in whom they have specialized, the magnitude of the special collections librarian's task falls into proper perspective. The logical corollary, implied by Gilliam, is that certain interesting manifestations of nineteenth-century book trading will never be properly examined because necessary collections will simply not exist. Further, in a more general literary sense, the career and writings of an important but prolific author like Sabine Baring-Gould will never be properly commented on. Gilliam's paper also emphasizes the role of the private collector and his relationship to institutional collections.

Robert Nikirk's paper shifts the focus on nineteenth-century books directly into the province of the collector. William Loring Andrews and Beverly Chew, as collectors, exemplified the bookish interests of an influential segment of American society, and this fascinating paper clearly shows the significance of their endeavors. Nikirk's paper is based on manuscript material held by the library of the Grolier Club, which has not previously been used for historical purposes. While it is perhaps difficult to determine exactly the way in which certain kinds of book collecting reflect contemporary taste, it is certainly true that the greatest research collections of books in North America are the direct result of private collecting zeal. A collector's taste can easily be determined if his collection survives intact in an institution. One of the most important points of Nikirk's paper, however, is that the libraries of his two subjects did not survive intact but were widely distributed. To reconstruct something of their connoisseurship is an important feat and a notable contribution to the history of collecting in America.

One other paper, not included in this volume, was presented to the Conference. In it Robert Stacey, a Canadian art historian, outlined a research problem utilizing nineteenth-century resources and illustrating it extensively with slides. His subject was William Cruikshank, an interesting, though minor, nineteenth-century artist of considerable importance to the book historian because much of Cruikshank's work first appeared in periodicals. Stacey reconstructed the life and career of Cruikshank from the printed and manuscript accounts that survive from the period and then subjected them to a close critical scrutiny. What emerged was a maze of confused identity, false trails, inaccurate information, and inadequate resources. Stacey's paper extended the theme of the conference into the realm of the researcher, whose plea for the proper treatment of nineteenth-century illustrated periodicals, including the indexing of art work, by special collections departments was noted by many of the conference delegates.

The conference dinner was held on the evening of June 16th and the address on that occasion was given by Stuart Schimmel, president of the Bibliographical Society of America and a well-known New York collector. His topic, yet another aspect of the nineteenth-century book world, was "On the shady side: the forger at work." While not a formal paper, Mr. Schimmel's remarks did present to the conference delegates several cogent observations on literary forgery, a topic of endless fascination. Mr. Schimmel was in the fortunate position of being able to provide his own primary resource material and, in the course of his talk, quoted extensively from letters in his own collection.

/ Literary forgers, he said, could be divided into two classes: the "amateurs" of the eighteenth century (he mentioned Psalmanazar, MacPherson, Chatterton, and Ireland) and the "professionals" of the nineteenth century. The former harmed mainly themselves while the latter "polluted the stream of scholarship." Schimmel highlighted his address with a consideration of three forgers: John Payne Collier, Major Byron (De Gibler), and Thomas J. Wise, their common attribute being their refusal to defend their actions and, when confronted by evidence of their forgeries, to deny any wrongdoing. Collier's explanation, in the face of incontrovertible evidence that the authorial emendations in his copy of the Shakespeare Second Folio had in fact been executed by himself (as quoted from a letter in Mr. Schimmel's collection), was that he was happy to be healthy enough in his old age to be able to reply to his critics. He did not, of course, ever reply. Major Byron, a self-styled illegitimate son of Lord Byron, perpetrated a whole series of forged letters of Byron and Shelley, letters which have bedeviled scholarship ever since. Faced with serious doubts concerning the authenticity of the letters, he retreated into what he referred to as "dignified silence and contempt." Wise, however, Schimmel said, took the prize. The numerous forgeries of nineteenth-century pamphlets attributed to him by Carter and Pollard were steadfastly denied by him. Schimmel quoted from three Wise letters written to people after the exposure of the forgeries and again the phrase "dignified silence" occurred.

The papers presented to the conference, and here presented in permanent form to a wider audience, emphasize two important general features of the nineteenth-century book trades: the revolutionary advances in the methods of producing and distributing books, and the dramatic increase in demand for books from a burgeoning reading public. It is perhaps ironic that the relative scarcity today of many popular nineteenth-century books should have been reiterated by several speakers. It is only in recent years that serious and sustained attention has been given to the literary products of the Victorian Age and much of the basic bibliographical and historical research remains to be done. The papers contributed to this volume provide fresh information and point the way for further investigation.

I would like to acknowledge the valuable editorial assistance of Desmond Neill, Librarian of Massey College at the University of Toronto, and the consistent support of Bill Matheson.

From Bookseller to Publisher: Changes in the London Book Trade, 1750-1850

Terry Belanger

Terry Belanger is an Assistant Professor, Columbia School of Library Service, Columbia University.

Although one cannot convincingly generalize about an entire century of book trade history on the basis of two examples, Thomas Longman I, born in 1699, and John Murray III, born in 1808, accurately symbolize some of the changes in the London book trade between 1750 and 1850.

In 1716, Thomas Longman, then seventeen years of age, was apprenticed to the London bookseller and publisher, John Osborn, who held the London agency for the distribution of Oxford bibles and who was a prominent publisher of works of practical instruction of all kinds. At the completion of his apprenticeship in 1724, Longman bought the shop of the recently deceased William Taylor, at the Ship in Paternoster Row, for somewhat more than £2200. He married his master's daughter, Mary Osborn, who was about eight years older than he; there were no children by the marriage. Osborn's own son, also named John, later joined Longman in the family business, but died young in 1734.

In 1746 Longman took as apprentice his fifteen-year-old nephew, Thomas Longman II; at the expiration of that apprenticeship in 1753, Thomas II was taken into partnership by his uncle. When Thomas I died in 1755, the imprints of Longman publications carried the name both of his widow and nephew until 1759; thereafter the name of Thomas II figured alone.[1]

---

1. The most accurate information about Thomas Longman and his successors is to be found in Philip Wallis, *At the Sign of the Ship: 1724-1974*. Printed for Private Circulation (London, Longman Group Ltd., 1974).

John Murray III, grandson of the founder of the celebrated publishing house, went to school in London and later to Edinburgh University, where his chief interests were in science, especially geology and mineralogy. He then studied languages abroad for a few years and in 1843, when his father, John Murray II, died, John III, aged 35, took over the firm, which he eventually bought from his mother.

In 1847 he married Marion Smith, the daughter of an Edinburgh banker. In 1851 he bought land in Wimbledon, to the south of London, and built a house; there he grew exotic rhododendrons as a hobby. He died in 1892 at the age of 83, leaving two sons to succeed him in the business.[2]

With these two examples in mind, the London book trade of the first half of the eighteenth century should be examined. In 1747, R. Campbell published a useful guide: *The London Tradesman. Being a Compendious View of All the Trades, Professions, Arts, both Liberal and Mechanic, now practised in the Cities of London and Westminster. Calculated for the Information of Parents, and Instruction of Youth in their Choice of Business.* Campbell states that the business of booksellers and publishers is

> to purchase original Copies [that is to say, copyrights] from Authors, to
> employ Printers to print them, and publish and sell them in their Shops;
> or to purchase Books from such as print them on their own Account, or
> at Auctions, and sell them at an advanced Price.[3]

The mid-eighteenth-century tradesman thus combined the modern functions of both publisher and retail bookseller. In his role as publisher, he could purchase literary material directly from authors. (A purchase was final, by the way: royalties were uncommon in 1750.) He could attend London sales open only to members of the trade at which the copyrights of deceased, retiring, or bankrupt publishers were offered for sale and he could buy shares in the copyrights of the steady, best-selling books of his day: dictionaries, popular works of practical instruction, classics of pastoral theology, standard school books, and so on. In his role as retail bookseller, he could exchange his own publications for those of other publishers, thus increasing the variety of books in his shop. He could also serve as retail agent for authors publishing their own books.

---

2. George Paston, *At John Murray's: 1843-1892* (London, John Murray, 1932).
3. R. Campbell, *The London Tradesman.* . . . (London, printed by T. Gardner, 1747), p. 128.

At mid-century many booksellers and publishers engaged in both whole-sale and retail trading were specialists: Mount and Page in nautical books, Rivington in theology, the Vaillants in foreign books, Tonson in literature, Walsh in music, Newbery in children's books, Cary in maps.

Another guide to the choice of trades, a contemporary of Campbell's *London Tradesman,* is J. Collier's 1761 *The Parents and Guardians Directory,* which provides a fairly detailed breakdown of mid-eighteenth-century bookselling. "The booksellers," he informs us,

> may be divided into the following classes: 1. The wholesale dealer, who subsists by his country trade, and by serving some of our plantations. 2. Those who deal only or principally in bibles, common prayers, almanacks, &c. who are also wholesale dealers. 3. The retale dealers, who generally deal in new books. 4. Those who deal chiefly in foreign books. 5. And those who sell old books.[4]

A young man with a small fortune of only 100 or 200 pounds, Collier continues, should not become an apprentice to a wholesale dealer,

> of whom he will learn nothing but the manner of packing up parcels, and the titles of those books for which there is the greatest demand in the country: As this is all he will learn in his apprenticeship, he will be almost as unfit to set up as a retail trader, as if he had been entirely unacquainted with bookselling; and not having a fortune to set up as a wholesale dealer, must be contented to be a journeyman.[5]

It is in the retail trade, Collier emphasizes, where "a sensible young man, of 1 or 200 1. fortune, has the fairest chance for improving it"—not in the wholesaling end of the trade, even though the "chief Riches and Profit" in the trade, Campbell reminds us, "is in the Property of valuable Copies," whether acquired at trade sales, by private treaty, or by direct contact with authors. Like Collier, Campbell makes a sharp distinction between apprentices with the capital resources enabling them to set up on their own as retailers at the end of their apprenticeships, and those without these resources:

> The Journeymen of this Trade have but a small Allowance. Fifteen or Twenty Pounds a Year is what is generally given. There is a Call but for few of these, and I apprehend the Trade in general overstocked; so that considering the Expence necessary to make a real understanding Book-

4. J. Collier, *The Parents and Guardians Directory* (London, 1761), p. 69.
5. Ibid., p. 70.

seller, and the Stock requisite to set him up, I cannot find much Encouragement for a Parent to design his Son to this Business.[6]

The risks of the book trade were touched upon by yet another mid-eighteenth-century guide to the choice of trades, the anonymous *General Description of All Trades,* also published in 1747. Many men, the *General Description of All Trades* observes,

have made handsome Fortunes in the Trade: Yet this is not to be done without running often-times great Risques, and having by them heavy Stocks of Books unsold; to alleviate which, they have a very prudent Method of several of them joining to carry on the larger Undertakings.[7]

Shared risk was one of the reasons for the share book system in the eighteenth-century London book trade. In looking at the nature of the membership in one of the more formal of these copyright-owning, loose trade associations, or *congers,* another reason becomes apparent: an attempt by a small, closely knit group of powerful London wholesalers to control the prices of books. An example is one of the congers described by Cyprian Blagden in *The Notebook of Thomas Bennet and Henry Clements.*[8] The Wholesaling Conger, at its height in about 1715, was an association of copyright-owning publishers who joined together for their mutual benefit in the face of uncertain legal copyright protection. Included among its members were Jacob Tonson, John Churchill, James Knapton, John Wyatt, Ranew Robinson, William Taylor (the man later bought out by Thomas Longman I), Henry Clements, John Osborn (the man to whom Longman was apprenticed), William Innys, and Jonas Brown. Note the connections among these men: In 1715 the Tonson firm was gradually being taken over by Jacob Tonson II, nephew of Jacob I. Later it was run by Jacob II's two sons, Jacob III and Richard. When Jacob III died in 1767, the firm was liquidated. John and Awnsham Churchill were the sons of a bookseller and were in partnership. Two of John's three sons went into the trade, one as a printer and the other as a stationer. James Knapton was apprenticed to Henry Mortlock, as was

6. Campbell, *London Tradesman,* pp. 134-35.

7. *A General Description of All Trades, Digested in Alphabetical Order: By Which Parents, Guardians, and Trustees, May . . . Make Choice of Trades Agreeable to the Capacity, Education, . . . and Fortune of the Youth Under Their Care* (London, Printed for T. Waller, 1747), p. 28.

8. Norma Hodgson and Cyprian Blagden, *The Notebook of Thomas Bennet and Henry Clements (1686-1719)* (Oxford, Oxford Bibliographical Society, 1956), pp. 67–85.

Edward Castle, who became the partner of one of John Churchill's sons. John Wyatt, apprenticed to Jonathan Robinson (the father of Ranew Robinson), died in the late 1720s. His firm was run for a time by an M. Wyatt, probably his widow, and then sold to Thomas Astley, who had been apprenticed to Henry Clements, another member of the Wholesaling Conger. Henry Clements, apprenticed to Thomas Bennet, who in turn had been apprenticed to Henry Mortlock, died in 1719 and was succeeded by William Innys, yet another member of the Wholesaling Conger.

These closely interwoven ties further emphasize what is very obvious regarding apprentice-master relationships, without mentioning marriage and other personal, local trade connections.

The one hundred years between the early eighteenth and early nineteenth centuries saw the substantial disintegration of these relationships and connections in the London book trade. One example of this disintegration was the breakdown of the congers themselves.

The Copyright Act of 1710 intended to establish legal terms during which copyrights could be held, after which the literary rights would go into the public domain. However, the Act failed to work, the main reasons being because the major London publishers throughout the first three-quarters of the eighteenth century insisted that common-law rights to literary property, like other property, were perpetual and could not be abridged by Parliament.[9]

In 1774, the matter was finally settled when the House of Lords abolished the validity of the principle of perpetual copyright, a decision of fundamental consequence for the subsequent history of the London and British book trades. As demonstrated by the failure of the 1710 Copyright Act, the London trade prior to 1774 had been divided into Insiders, who owned copyrights, and Outsiders, who were not major share book copyright holders and who were frequently prevented from acquiring any.

For several decades after the 1774 decision ending perpetual copyright, the major London copyright holders worked together and continued to issue jointly published editions of popular share books, relying on their collectively superior trade relationships with country and colonial booksellers to maintain a near monopoly over these titles, even though they were out of copyright. But the system broke down. While it is not uncom-

---

9. Terry Belanger, "Booksellers' Sales of Copyright: Aspects of the London Book Trade 1718–1768" (Ph.D. diss., Columbia University, 1970), chapter 6. *See also* Gwyn Walters, "The Booksellers in 1759 and 1774: The Battle for Literary Property," *The Library*, 5th ser. 29 (Sept. 1974); 287–311.

mon to see a London-published book of the 1770s with ten, twenty, even forty booksellers' names at the bottom of the title page, by the middle of the nineteenth century the practice began to cease and one, or at most a few, publishers' names appeared on London imprints.

Another reason for the disintegration of a closely knit London trade was the changing relationship between London, and country and colonial retail booksellers. One of the great difficulties in doing business in the provinces in the first half of the eighteenth century was the shortage of hard money. The bookseller in Lichfield, for example, needed books from London, but he had nothing to send to the London bookseller acting as his agent in payment for these books when hard currency was scarce and when there were virtually no banking services of any kind in his own neighborhood. A complicated system of bills of exchange had to be worked out, whereby the Lichfield bookseller might send his London agent payment in the form of bills of exchange sent from London to one of his Lichfield neighbors—perhaps a cattle drover who had sent a herd of beef cattle up to London for sale to a Smithfield butcher. This complicated system could be made to work, but only with some difficulty: it relied completely on personal acquaintance and trust built up over a number of years.

But in the second half of the eighteenth century, provincial banks began to open and financial facilities became much more common in the country. The provincial bookseller could pay for London purchases with bills drawn on his local bank, bills which the London bookseller could then deposit in his own account. While it is difficult to imagine what commerce would be like without banks and an easily available currency, until the 1760s, and in the more remote areas of Great Britain until much later, banking facilities of any kind were either primitive or totally absent.

The consequences of the easy and impersonal exchange of funds are notable. A Lichfield retail bookseller could now order books from any publisher in London. Not only would there be no difficulty in getting his bills accepted by the London publishers, but the latter began sending commercial travelers into the provinces, carrying samples and registering sales, either before or after the publication of the London firm's new and back list. Indeed, with the development of paved roads, fast coaches, canals, and soon, railways, communication between London and the country was becoming increasingly simple. London publishers began developing national connections, but at the expense of local ones.

Another major disintegrating influence on the London trade in the second half of the eighteenth century was caused by the enormous demand for books by a rapidly growing, increasingly literate population. Note how James Lackington capitalized on this demand, accumulating a large stock of books which he sold at low prices. "It was some time in the year seventeen hundred and eighty," he tells us,

> when I resolved from that period to give no person whatever any credit. I was introduced to make this resolution from various motives: I had observed, that where credit was given, most bills were not paid within six months, many not within a twelve month, and some not within two years. Indeed, many tradesmen have accounts of seven years standing; and some bills are never paid. The losses sustained by the interest of money in long credits, and by those bills that were not paid at all; the inconveniences attending not having the ready-money to lay out in trade to the best advantage, together with the great loss to time in keeping accounts, and collecting debts, convinced me, that if I could but establish a ready-money business, *without any exceptions,* I should be enabled to sell every article very cheap. When I communicated my ideas on this subject to some of my acquaintances, I was much laughed at and ridiculed; and it was thought, that I might as well attempt to rebuild the tower of Babel, as to establish a large business without giving credit. But notwithstanding this discouragement . . . I determined to make the experiment; and began by marking in every book the lowest price that I would take for it; which being much lower than the common market prices, I not only retained my former customers, but soon increased their numbers.[10]

For many years Lackington's relations with his colleagues were unfriendly because of his practice of buying up books and then remaindering them. He was breaking established trade customs, but by the end of the eighteenth century the London book trade was an insufficiently cohesive body to stop him: individual enterprise prevailed over traditional methods of doing business.

In his *London Tradesman* of 1747, R. Campbell had emphasized that the "chief Riches and Profit" in the trade was "in the Property of valuable Copies." But here was Lackington, keeping his carriage on the profits of a retail business. In this shift is seen another aspect of the disintegration of a unified, tightly knit London book trade: a new method of accumulating large amounts of capital with which to begin publishing ventures.

---

10. James Lackington, *Memoirs of the First Forty-Five Years of the Life of James Lackington.* New ed., corr. and much enl. (London, printed for the author, 1792), pp. 335–36.

Graham Pollard illustrates this development in his 1959 Sandars Lectures with a reference to the first edition of *Leigh's New Picture of London*, 1818.[11] The chapter on the "General State of Literature and the Fine Arts of London" lists several varieties of booksellers and publishers. They include:

1. Wholesale Booksellers and Publishers who supply the town and country trade, and execute foreign orders of every description.
2. Wholesale Booksellers and Publishers who chiefly confine themselves to their own publications.
3. Retail Booksellers and Publishers.

As examples of wholesale booksellers and publishers who chiefly confine themselves to their own publications, Leigh lists Cadell and Davies and John Murray, both firms with solid eighteenth-century roots. Cadell and Davies in particular trace their ancestry directly back to the house founded by Andrew Millar in the 1730s. But as Pollard points out, it is not true that the publisher evolved solely from the share bookowning bookseller. Many nineteenth-century firms got their start as retail establishments which only eventually, as profits began accumulating, began to publish books.

Still another new route to publishing to which little attention has been paid is the antiquarian book trade. The only requirement for setting up as an antiquarian bookseller was money—trade connections were not needed either to buy or sell old books. Take, for instance, the case of William Pickering as recounted by Sir Geoffrey Keynes in his memoir of this celebrated publisher:

> It is stated that 'his father was a book-loving earl and his mother a lady of title'. . . . His name was derived from that of a tailor called Pickering with whose wife he was put out to nurse. . . . In 1810, when he was fourteen years old, he was placed as an apprentice with John and Arthur Arch, the Quaker booksellers and publishers, whose business was at 61 Cornhill on the Bishopsgate corner. This arrangement may have been made through the interest of his noble father. The fact that some of the earliest books afterwards published by Pickering, beginning with the Diamond Classics edition of *Virgil*, 1821, have on their title-pages the coat of arms of Earl Spencer (second earl, 1758-1834), followed by a dedication to him, is perhaps sufficient indication of the source of both his life and fortune.[12]

11. Graham Pollard, "The English Market for Printed Books." (Typescript in the University Library, Cambridge, 1959 Sandars Lectures), p. 33.

12. Sir Geoffrey Keynes, *William Pickering, Publisher: A Memoir and a Checklist of His Publications*. Rev. ed. (London, The Galahad Press, 1969), p. 9.

A few years after Pickering came of age, he set up on his own in Lincoln's Inn Fields. "One or other of his parents retained an interest in his welfare," continues Sir Geoffrey, "and at this juncture a thousand pounds was very opportunely placed to his credit at the bank."[13] Pickering evidently intended to concentrate on the sale of second-hand and antiquarian books, an interest he never abandoned even when he became a substantial publisher of new editions.

Now the early decades of the nineteenth century saw bibliomania descend upon Great Britain. Fortunes could be and were made in the antiquarian book trade, allowing many men amass the capital to set up as publishers, where there were still greater profits to be made. William Blackwood of Edinburgh established the foundations of his famous publishing firm in this fashion, as did Adam Black; even the Longmans opened an antiquarian book department.

Earlier it was suggested that booksellers in the first half of the eighteenth century tended to come from book trade families, to serve a full apprenticeship, to marry into the trade, to be possessed of at least some capital with which to begin business on their own, to maintain close personal and trade relationships in London, to enjoy the exclusive or nearly exclusive agency for various country and colonial retail booksellers, to prefer to publish steady best-selling books jointly as part of the share book system, to live over their shops, and to put their sons to apprentice in the book trades. This profile is reflected in a letter written in 1717 by Alexander Pope. Riding to Oxford one day, Pope writes, he was overtaken by

> the enterprizing Mr. *Lintott,* the redoutable rival of Mr. *Tonson.* . . . I enquir'd of his son. "The lad (says he) has fine parts, but is somewhat sickly, *much as you are*—I spare for nothing in his education at *Westminster.* . . . I hope the boy will make his fortune."
> Don't you design to let him pass a year at *Oxford*? "To what purpose? (said he) the Universities do but make Pedants, and I intend to breed him a man of Business."[14]

Certainly, a century later, many changes had taken place. The trade became much larger, and the distinction between retail bookseller, publisher, and wholesaler of the books of many publishers became clearer. Individual firms tended to publish on their own account, rather than in partnership with several other publishers. The development of national banking and transportation systems enabled wider though less intimate

13. Ibid., p. 10.
14. Alexander Pope, *Correspondence of Alexander Pope,* ed. George Sherburn (Oxford, Oxford University Press, 1956), vol. I, p. 371.

relationships with a much larger group of retailers spread over a much greater territory. The separation of the retail bookseller from the publisher caused more competition in both sectors. Authors earned more, and they were as likely to prefer royalties on their writings as lump-sum payments for their copyrights. The publisher and the author increasingly found themselves in a continuing, professional partnership in the promotion and sale of books, which were now cheaper because of technological advances in papermaking, printing, binding, and illustration, and because of the economies of scale caused by larger size editions.

Publishers became as deeply concerned with periodicals as they were with books, and *Magazine Day,* the end-of-the-month distribution of London-based periodicals to the country, became a recurring and chaotic feature of life in Paternoster Row, which remained the geographical heart of the London book trade even though the publisher no longer lived over the shop but rather became a commuter. Offspring may eventually enter the firm, but they will receive a good education, including university training, first and are as likely to marry outside of the book trade as in. Times have, in short, moved from a Thomas Longman I to a John Murray III.

It could, perhaps, be argued though that John Murray III was not a strictly typical London bookseller and publisher, since he was a member of a great book-trade dynasty. However, other, more ordinary, examples are plentiful: for instance, Daniel Macmillan. Born in 1813, he was a Scots peasant who came to London at age twenty, scratched a living as a clerk in a retail shop in London and Cambridge to accumulate capital, and eventually began to publish books. He had no London trade connections except those he forged himself, but he had intelligence, some education, and ambition—and, most importantly, the ability to adjust to quickly changing trade conditions and to profit by them. Flexibility seems to be the chief quality which distinguishes the John Duntons from the James Lackingtons, the eighteenth-century booksellers from the nineteenth-century publishers.

The Publishing of Children's Books in Victoria's Day

Judith St. John

Judith St. John is Head of the Osborne and Lillian H. Smith Collections of Children's Literature at the Toronto Public Libraries.

The publishing history of English children's books written between 1810-1910 is indeed an interesting one. However, to compress a century of publishing for children into limited space seems a difficult assignment and I have, therefore, decided to concentrate on Victoria's Day, defining that as the first forty-two years of her long life, from the year of her birth in 1819, to the death of Prince Albert, her consort, in 1861. (I regret that some important firms such as the two Darton firms and the Religious Tract Society will not receive the attention they deserve.)

Many of the prominent publishers of 1819 had been in business for many years and I hope to survey briefly the first two decades of the century. While it is a temptation to spend all my time on these years, I also wish to show how the children's books published during the next twenty years might have been largely responsible for the people who grew into the rather stodgy, stuffy adults identified by some as Victorians, and how forward-looking publishers produced books in the 1840s and 50s that set free the minds and imaginations of children who grew up to create in the last four decades of the century what has been termed the "Golden Age of Children's Literature."

The publishers and booksellers of the nineteenth century were, as are their present-day counterparts, the ultimate censors of the world of books. It was they who rejected the manuscripts they believed would not sell; determined what books would be allowed to go out of print; often en-

17

couraged writers, provided ideas, edited faltering prose, and decided on illustrations and formats. Nineteenth-century publishers also engaged in competition but published volumes jointly, sold one another's books in their bookshops, and even advertised rival series. Many firms were intertwined by marriage. They were a little lower than the gentry, a little higher than the trade.

Today's publishers have promotion and public relations officers and book jackets to carry blurbs and advertisements. But in the nineteenth century the publisher or writer often advertised other available titles within the text of a book, or added pages of publishers' advertisements, often annotated and, in the latter part of the century, illustrated. Often the publishers used these pages for dispensing information to members of the trade or to libraries. At the end of *First Going to School* (1804), the Tabart Juvenile Library gave notice to country booksellers of assortments available at six months credit with the option of exchanging unsaleable items.[1] The Religious Tract Society offered circulating libraries "169 volumes to subscribers for £12, 8s. 6d. with a library case with folding doors, lock and key, neatly painted (18s.), packing case for ditto (4s.); hints on circulating libraries, rules and catalogues and a librarian's book, gratis."[2] The Darton firm sometimes inserted an engraved advertising leaf. The Whittaker firm published in 1839 Knott's *New Aid to Memory,* dedicated to Her Most Gracious Majesty, Queen Victoria, with a list of subscribers headed by Her Most Gracious Majesty, the Queen Dowager (Queen Adelaide). At the end was a surprising advertisement for an "Indian Dentifrice," sold by the London Benevolent Society, "used by the late Queen Charlotte and . . . adopted by the Royal Family and a large portion of the nobility and gentry."[3] Publishers often included "Advertisements" as prefaces or introductions such as the preliminary page in *Dame Partlet's Farm* (1804):

> At Harris's, St. Paul's Churchyard,
> Good children meet a sure reward;
> In coming home the other day

1. Dorothy Kilner [M. Pelham], *First Going to School; or The Story of Tom Brown, and His Sisters* (London, Tabart and Co., 1804), p. 121.

2. John Bunyan, *The Barren Fig-Tree; or, The Doom and Downfall of the Fruitless Professor: Shewing Some of the Signs by Which Such a Character may be Known* (London, The Religious Tract Society [1831?]), p. 1 of publisher's advertisements at end.

3. Robert Rowe Knott [pseud.], *The New Aid to Memory. Part the First, Containing the Most Remarkable Events of the History of England* (London, Whittaker and Co., 1839). Advertisement bound in at end.

I heard a little master say,
For ev'ry penny there he took
He had receiv'd a little book,
With covers neat, and cuts so pretty,
There's not its like in all the city;
And that for two-pence he could buy
A story-book would make one cry;
For little more a book of riddles:
Then let us not buy drums or fiddles,
Nor yet be stopt at pastry-cooks,
But spend our money all on books.[4]

Princess Victoria was born on May 24, 1819, the year before the death of King George III who had reigned for sixty years. During that same month, John Harris, the eminent bookseller and publisher of the Juvenile Library in St. Paul's Church-Yard, took his son into partnership. The advertisement in the 1819 edition of Mrs. Hofland's *Blind Farmer* lists thirty-six books and ends with the note:

> J. Harris and Son beg leave to apprise the Public, that their Library is not confined to Publications of their own; but that every Book or Device calculated to enlarge the Minds, or correct the Morals of their Young Friends, may be purchased at the Old Establishment, St. Paul's Church-Yard.[5]

The elder John Harris was born in 1756 and had attained his freedom from apprenticeship through service in 1780. He worked for the firms of Thomas Evans and John Murray before entering the firm of Elizabeth Newbery, the widow of Francis Newbery, the nephew of John Newbery who had commenced his Juvenile Library in 1744. John Harris was Elizabeth's manager from 1797 until her retirement in 1801, when he took over the stock and assets of her firm. He continued his predecessor's competition with John Marshall who had achieved his freedom just two years before John Harris but had been from 1782 publishing under his own imprint such popular authors as Lady Fenn, Dorothy Kilner, and Mrs. Trimmer. John Marshall had been the Printer to the Cheap Repository, began in 1795 by Hannah More, Wilberforce, Zachary Macaulay, and others in their successful effort to provide cheap material with

---

4. *Dame Partlet's Farm; Containing an Account of the Great Riches She Obtained by Industry, the Good Life She Led, and Alas, Good Reader! Her Sudden Death; to Which is Added a Hymn, Written by Dame Partlet, Just before Her Death, and an Epitaph for Her Tombstone* (London, J. Harris, 1804), p. 3.

5. Barbara (Wreaks) Hoole Hofland, *The Blind Farmer and His Children*, 2nd ed. (London, Harris and Son, 1819), p. 8 of publisher's advertisements at end.

evangelical content for the poor and the young. It was disbanded in 1798 and the Religious Tract Society was formed the following year. According to M. G. Jones's biography, Hannah More had disliked and distrusted Marshall because she felt his treatment of Sarah Trimmer had been ungenerous. "Mr. Marshall has never belied my first impression of him," she wrote, "selfish, tricking, and disobliging from first to last."[6] In spite of Mrs. More's harsh opinion, John Marshall continued to prosper and an E. Marshall (possibly Eleanor) continued to publish forty-six years after John had began his business.

John Harris has been likened to old John Newbery. Mrs. Moon quotes a review in the *Gentleman's Magazine* (November, 1817):

> We have frequently had occasion to mention the name of this worthy Publisher, as the genuine successor of the benevolent and intelligent Mr. John Newbery, famed in *olden times* for his judicious selection of Books of rational Amusement for the rising generation. Steadily pursuing the same laudable exertions, new books, for the entertainment and instruction of youth, are continually issuing from the Corner of St. Paul's Church-Yard, calculated, we conscientiously assert, to form the morals and fix the religious principles of the juvenile Reader.[7]

Like his famous predecessor, John Harris had a merry sense of humor. He brought a new levity to children's books when he published a trilogy, *The Comic Adventures of Old Mother Hubbard and her Dog* on June 1, 1805, with a *Continuation* on January 1, 1806, and a *Sequel* on March 1, 1806. On January 1, 1807, he published a poem, *The Butterfly's Ball and the Grasshopper's Feast,* written by William Roscoe, a Member of Parliament, an attorney, botanist, historian, and book collector. It had first appeared in November, 1806, in the *Gentleman's Magazine,* of which John Harris was a proprietor. When published with illustrations by William Mulready, it precipitated a rash of sequels and imitations brought out by many publishers. Roscoe's *Butterfly's Birth-day,* printed in 1809 by Longman, Hurst, Rees, and Orme, and John Harris, advertises *The Butterfly's Ball* and Mrs. Dorset's *Peacock "At Home"* on the back cover: "A better proof cannot be given of the estimation in which these little works have been held by the public, than the assurance

6. Mary Gwladys Jones, *Hannah More* (Cambridge, Cambridge University Press, 1952), p. 143.

7. Marjorie Moon, *John Harris's Books for Youth, 1801-1843* (Cambridge, Marjorie Moon in association with Five Owl Press Limited and Alan Spilman [1976]), p. 5.

of the publisher, that, together, nearly forty thousand copies ! ! ! have been sold in twelve months."[8]

In 1819 when John Harris's son entered partnership, they published a new series in a larger format under the same title: "Harris's Cabinet of Amusement and Instruction." Many of the earlier books were reprinted, one of which was *Peter Piper's Practical Principles of Plain and Perfect Pronunciation,* first published in 1813. *Peter Piper's* Polite Preface began: "Peter Piper Puts Pen to Paper to Produce his Peerless Production, Proudly Presuming it will Please Princes, Peers and Parliaments."[9] When an American edition was published in 1830 it was impossible to have "Princes, Peers and Parliaments." It was changed to please the "Palettes of Pretty Prattling Playfellows." An article against such ridiculous books was published in an 1820 issue of the *London Magazine,* naming the firm of John Harris and Son as "great offenders . . . what excuse can they offer to the rising, and risen generations, for publishing that vile book called—'Peter Piper's Practical Principles'?" The author referred to the stanza:

> Lanky Lawrence lost his Lass and Lobster;
> Did Lanky Lawrence lose his Lass and Lobster?
> If Lanky Lawrence lost his Lass and Lobster,
> Where are the Lass and Lobster Lanky Lawrence lost?[10]

The writer called it "degrading trash . . . a delicate morsel of nick-names, gallantry, and gluttony to enrich a child's mind with." He went on to denounce John Marshall's *The Dandies Ball,* also published in 1819, with its "nonsense, buffoonery and ribaldry . . . and its glaring coloured prints [which] assist the corrupting tendency of the composition."[11]

Undaunted, the Harris firm published in 1820 *The History of the Sixteen Wonderful Old Women, Illustrated by as Many Engravings, Exhibiting Their Principal Eccentricities and Amusements.* It is the first known book of limericks, published twenty-six years before Edward Lear brought out his limericks. However, it was John Marshall's book of *Anecdotes and Adventures of Fifteen Gentlemen,* published about 1822,

8. William Roscoe, *The Butterfly's Birth-day* (London, Longman, Hurst, Rees, and Orme, and J. Harris [1809]), back cover.

9. *Peter Piper's Practical Principles of Plain and Perfect Pronunciation. To Which is Added, a Collection of Moral and Entertaining Conundrums* (London, J. Harris and Son, 1820), p. 9.

10. Ibid., p. 18.

11. Moon, *John Harris's Books for Youth,* p. 158.

that Lear knew as a child and acknowledged as his inspiration. He claimed that the limerick beginning "There was an old man of Tobago" was his favorite.

John Marshall was not the only firm to take advantage of John Harris's imagination, enterprise, and acumen. On September 25, 1820, Harris and Son published *The Path of Learning Strewed with Flowers, or English Grammar Illustrated.* In 1821 John Marshall's *The Path of Learning Strewed with Roses, or The Elements of English Grammar* appeared. Soon after, *The Road of Learning Strewed with Flowers, or Child's First Book* was published by Dean and Munday and A. K. Newman and Co. All had brightly hand-colored illustrations.

The firm of Dean & Munday had its beginnings in the eighteenth century. It is thought that the partners served their apprenticeships with the Bailey firm that carried on a publishing business at the "Sign, Great A, Little a, Bouncing B." Both Dean and Munday married daughters of Thomas Bailey. They entered into partnership and resided over their business premises on Threadneedle Street. The families were so closely integrated that even their silverware was initialed D. & M. As well as publishing children's books, Dean & Munday were famous for their valentines and did all the printing for the East India Company.

The Dean firm became closely associated with Anthony King Newman who had been in business with William Lane. Lane was a poulterer's son who began selling books in his father's shop, prospered as a bookseller and publisher, established the famous Minerva Press in 1790, and was instrumental in founding circulating libraries "in almost every town and village" throughout the country. Newman succeeded Lane as head of the Minerva Press in 1809. In his Introduction to *Deborah Dent and Her Donkey,* published by Dean & Munday in 1823, and reprinted in 1887 in the "Leadenhall Press Series of Forgotten Picture Books for Children," Andrew W. Tuer records the publishing arrangements that existed between Dean & Munday and A. K. Newman: "Of those [books] that pleased him Newman was in the habit of ordering, at half the published price, special editions of one thousand copies, wherein the imprint of Dean & Munday, Threadneedle Street, was dropped and his own substituted. When copies were ordered in small quantities only, as required, this arrangement was departed from, and the joint imprint used of Dean & Munday, Threadneedle Street, and A. K. Newman & Co., Leadenhall Street."[12] Newman was shrewd enough to realize that he would sell more than a thousand copies of *Dame Wiggins of Lee, and Her*

12. *Deborah Dent and Her Donkey. A Humorous Tale* (London, Field & Tuer, 1887), pp. ii-iii.

Seven Wonderful Cats. A Humorous Tale. Written Principally by a Lady of Ninety. The Osborne Collection holds the first edition of 1823 with the imprint of A. K. Newman & Co. The original verses have been ascribed to R. S. Sharpe, the grocer to whom *Anecdotes and Adventures of Fifteen Gentlemen* has also been attributed. The lady of ninety has been identified as a Mrs. Pearson who conducted a toy shop. John Ruskin acclaimed *Dame Wiggins* as his favorite children's book and brought out a facsimile edition in 1885 with his own additional verses and a few new illustrations by Kate Greenaway.

The Dean firm also published books that had been initiated by A. K. Newman. W. F. Sullivan's *The Young Liar! ! A Tale of Truth and Caution; for the Benefit of the Rising Generation* was published by A. K. Newman & Co. in 1818. Three years later Dean & Munday published it under the title *Young Wilfred, or The Punishment of Falsehood.* The delinquent Wilfred's library "mostly consisted of romances . . . the fairy tales of the Countes d'Anois, Persian Tales, Valentine and Orson, Arabian Nights and *Gulliver's Travels,* books either too frivolous, improper or incomprehensible, for children." Wilfred, at the age of nine, enrolled in the academy of Dr. Birchall, a stern disciplinarian, who considered plays an abomination and "would as soon see the scarlet-fever as a play-book in school." He maintained that "even Shakespeare himself was his aversion, and he often declared, he wished the fellow had never been born."[13] Dr. Birchall's influence did not cure Wilfred's propensity for telling "guileful fibs" that ultimately led to his ignominious death in a duel.

The ending of this book would not have met with the approval of the Quaker firm of Darton and Harvey that had been publishing from 55 Gracechurch Street since 1791. In a book of short stories published in 1828, the publisher (then Harvey and Darton) lamented that many of the works written for youth were "too exciting—too much in the style of novels." Maria Hack, whose daughter married John Maw Darton, would have also disapproved of Wilfred's library, for she wrote in her preface to *Winter Evenings or Tales of Travellers:* "Stories of giants and castles do not accord with the taste of the present day . . . and an unlimited perusal of them will exhaust the sensibility, and produce the same listless indifference to the realities of life, observable in older persons, who devote their time to this kind of reading."[14]

13. William Francis Sullivan, *The Young Liar!! A Tale of Truth and Caution; for the Benefit of the Rising Generation* (London, A. K. Newman & Co., 1818), pp. 8, 25.

14. Maria (Barton) Hack, *Winter Evenings; or Tale of Travellers* (London, Darton, Harvey, and Darton, 1818-20, vol. I, pp. iii-iv.

Although Grimm's fairy tales were translated into English by Edgar Taylor in 1823, fairy tales and nursery rhymes soon became available only in chapbook form. Provincial publishers such as Rusher of Banbury, Kendrew of York, and Richardson of Derby produced these stories in cheap little booklets, penny plain or twopence colored, light enough to be carried in peddlars' packs or by pedestrian booksellers.

In 1824, the elder John Harris retired from business and levity in children's books began to disappear. His sober son, John, a true man of his time, conducted the business alone for the next nineteen years. He continued to publish the "Cabinet of Amusement and Instruction" series, but in the late twenties he changed the name to one more acceptable to the time: "Harris's 1s 6d Books Coloured." He dropped from the series *Peter Piper's Practical Principles* (perhaps he had been influenced by the unkind reference to that popular book).

The publishing principles of John Harris II were set forth in the preface of M. E. Budden's *Key to Knowledge; or, Things in common use simply and shortly explained:* "To gratify, without misleading; to meet curiosity with satisfactory explanation; to inform, without confounding; to instruct, without fatiguing."[15] Harris continued to publish the popular series of travel books for "Tarry-at-home Travellers" by the Reverend Isaac Taylor of Ongar, the father of Ann and Jane Taylor. The books in this series appeared in many editions and with many revisions.

Christina Duff Stewart in her two-volume analytical bio-bibliography of the Taylors of Ongar (published by Garland in 1974) mentions a review in the *Gentleman's Magazine* of *Scenes in Europe* which reported that "an impression of 3000 copies was disposed of in about nine months after its first publication." This must have been an unusually high sale because an advertisement at the back of an 1819 Harris publication praises Elizabeth Sandham's *The Twin Sisters, or The Advantages of Religion,* and notes that its success has been far beyond the author's and publisher's expectations, twelve thousand copies having been disposed of in fourteen years

During the late 1820s and early 1830s there was a spate of travel and natural history books or stories condemning the slave trade, race prejudice, and class distinction. The publisher, John Arliss, in an advertisement at the end of Mr. Frankly's *Trial of Harry Hardheart; for Ingratitude and Cruelty to Certain Individuals of the Brute Creation* assured

---

15. Mary Elizabeth (Halsey) Budden [pseud.], *Key to Knowledge; or Things in Common Use Simply and Shortly Explained.* By a mother . . . 10th ed. (London, John Harris, 1837), p. vii.

"parents, guardians, and tutors in general . . . that every sentence of an immoral or improper nature, is carefully expunged" from the books sold in his juvenile library.

These sentiments were shared by the firms that catered especially to the evangelical market. One of these was F. Houlston and Son of Wellington, Salop, which had begun in the eighteenth century but from 1800 was carried on by the widow, Frances Houlston, and her son, Edward. They printed sermons and tracts and were fortunate enough to publish Mrs. Sherwood's first book, *The History of Little Henry and His Bearer* (1814), which had been written in India. Its publication coincided with the growing interest in the missionary movement and the book maintained a constant popularity for the rest of the century. Its popularity has been compared to that of *Uncle Tom's Cabin*. It has been estimated that Mrs. Sherwood wrote approximately 350 books and tracts, and the Houlston firm printed a large share of these titles. With the tracts of Mrs. Sherwood and her sister, Mrs. Cameron, the prosperity of the firm was assured. Hatchards was their London agent until 1818 when they became the publishers of Mrs. Sherwood's most famous book, *The History of the Fairchild Family*.

Hatchards of Piccadilly (still in existence), was the chief publisher and bookseller of the Clapham Evangelicals. John Hatchard began his business in 1797 with five pounds of his own and died in 1849 with an estate of nearly one hundred thousand pounds. He has been described as the "acme of respectability, dressed in semi-clerical style with an unvarying gracious manner, and patience under the martyrdom of gout." In 1833 he published Mrs. Mortimer's *Peep of Day: or, A Series of the Earliest Religious Instruction the Infant Mind is Capable of Receiving*. It was widely translated into many languages including French, German, Russian, Samoan, and Chinese. The Osborne Collection holds the edition published by Hatchards in 1886 with "Seven hundred and thirty-fourth thousand" on the title page. A sequel, *Line upon Line,* published in two volumes in 1837 and 1838, had sold 1,400,000 copies when the Osborne edition was published fifty years later. Hatchard is said to have been the first to use lithographs in a children's book. The process had been introduced to England in 1817 by Rudolph Ackerman, described as enterprising and amiable, "one of the most industrious and honorable of the literary fraternity." The organization of Friends of the Osborne and Lillian H. Smith Collections has reprinted his *Healthful Sports for Young Ladies,* published in 1822.

Hannah More was well known at Hatchards. They published some of her earlier works including an edition of *The Shepherd of Salisbury Plain* which had first appeared as a Cheap Repository Tract in 1795. This popular book had many American editions and was read as a child by Samuel Griswold Goodrich, born in 1793, the son of a Connecticut Congregational minister. He records in his two-volume autobiography, *Recollections of a lifetime,* that he read no books until he was ten. At the age of twelve he read *Robinson Crusoe* and Hannah More's *Shepherd of Salisbury Plain.* He wrote that from the latter highly moral tale he had received his first glimpse of the joys of reading.[16] Goodrich established his own publishing house in Hartford in 1818. Five years later he visited England and made a pilgrimage to meet Hannah More who at that time was a woman of seventy-nine. Goodrich regarded her as one of the greatest benefactors of the age and one of the most remarkable women who had ever lived. Through his conversations with Mrs. More his belief was strengthened that facts could be made more interesting than fiction. He had, he told her, "long entertained the idea of making a reform in books for youth." After his return home he wrote *Tales of Peter Parley about America,* which he published anonymously in 1827 for, as he acknowledged in 1855, "nursery literature had not acquired the respect in the world it now enjoys." He gave up publishing and wrote five or six books a year. In thirty years he had written one hundred seventy books of which he estimated seven million copies had been sold. In 1932, F. J. Harvey Darton, in his *Children's Books in England,* wrote: "Probably no juvenile author has ever had so large a circulation of so many books in so short a time."

A host of counterfeit and pirated editions of Peter Parley books appeared and the most offensive were in England. Thomas Tegg, said to have been the wealthiest bibliopole in the United Kingdom, was the most serious offender. He had begun business at the turn of the century, purchased bankrupt stocks and remainders, and was described as a "literary undertaker" on a large scale. He held nightly auctions in his crowded premises at 73 Cheapside. When Goodrich was in England in 1832 he found one of his books on Tegg's press. Tegg told Goodrich that his books, as they were written, were not acceptable in England, so Goodrich offered to revise them and drew up a contract whereby he would be paid ten pounds for every thousand copies. Goodrich revised fourteen books but heard nothing from Tegg for ten years. When Goodrich visited him in

16. Samuel Griswold Goodrich, *Recollections of a Lifetime; or, Men and Things I Have Seen* (New York & Auburn, Miller, Orton, & Co., 1857), vol. I, pp. 172-3.

England in 1842 (when Dickens was touring America to complain about the piracies of his books), Tegg told him the document was not valid: "Sir, I do not owe you a farthing—neither justice nor law require me to pay you anything." However, Tegg finally paid him four hundred pounds and Goodrich received no more from Tegg or his successors.

Charles Tilt who had been an assistant of Hatchards, began his own business in 1827. He published *Peter Parley's Visit to London, During the Coronation of Queen Victoria* (1838). Goodrich wrote plaintively in his autobiography: "I have no objection to Englishmen singing 'Rule Britannia' but it is most unpleasant to find it in a book the world believes is by an American."

The worthy Darton firm published genuine Parley books by arrangement, although they were guilty of publishing for distribution in America. They also published spurious Peter Parley books, many of which were written by Samuel Clark, partner and brother-in-law of J. M. Darton, under the pseudonym, Reverend T. Wilson. Goodrich paid Clark, who eventually became a priest, the compliment of admitting that his *Peter Parley's Wonders of Earth, Sea, and Sky* was the only English counterfeit he would have cared to acknowledge. An English periodical, *Peter Parley's Magazine,* was published monthly and in annual volumes from 1840–92 first by Simpkin and Marshall, and from 1844–68 by the Darton firm, edited by William Martin, who as a poor boy had been befriended and educated by Elizabeth Fry.

The word "Parleyize" had become a common word by 1838 when Tegg in his "Address of the Publishers" for *Tales About Christmas by Peter Parley* wrote: "We wish that we could thoroughly *Parleyize* the rising generation, not only for our own interest, but, also, for their advantage."[17]

The effect of this diet of reading on England's children alarmed Catherine Sinclair, who wrote in her preface to *Holiday House* (1839):

> In these pages the author has endeavoured to paint that species of noisy, frolicsome, mischievous children, now almost extinct, wishing to preserve a sort of fabulous remembrance of days long past, when young people were like horses on the prairies, rather than like well-broken hacks on the road; and when amidst many faults and eccentricities, there was still some individuality of character and feeling allowed to remain.[18]

---

17. George Mogridge [pseud.], *Tales about Christmas by Peter Parley* (London, Thomas Tegg and Son, 1838), p. xxiii.

18. Catherine Sinclair, *Holiday House: a Series of Tales* (Edinburgh, William Whyte and Co., 1844), p. vii.

Several people recognized the dire consequences of didactic reading. One was Joseph Cundall, who in 1834 as a boy of sixteen had entered the firm of Charles Tilt and at the age of twenty-two had succeeded Nathaniel Hailes. Hailes, when in partnership with John Sharpe at the Juvenile Library at the London Museum, had published, anonymously, *Sir Horn-book; or Childe Launcelot's Expedition, a Grammatico-Allegorical Ballad* written by Thomas Love Peacock. The firm was noted for its fine printing.

Ruari McLean suggests in his biography of Joseph Cundall that Cundall might have met Henry Cole at Hailes's Juvenile Library when buying books for his eight children. This may be true but it seems more likely that the introduction would have been made through Cole's close personal friend, Thomas Love Peacock. Cole, who adopted the pseudonym Felix Summerly, asked the young Cundall to publish a series to be known as *The Home Treasury*. The booklets were printed by Charles Whittingham, the younger, at the Chiswick Press, which had the reputation of being one of the best printing establishments in the world. The original announcement for "Felix Summerly's Home Treasury of Books, Pictures, Toys, &c." may be familiar:

> The character of most Children's Books published during the last quarter of a century, is fairly typified in the name of Peter Parley, which the writers of some hundreds of them have assumed. The books themselves have been addressed after a narrow fashion almost entirely to the cultivation of the understanding of children. The many tales sung or said from time immemorial, which appealed to the other, and certainly not less important elements of a child's mind, its fancy, imagination, sympathies, affections, are almost all gone out of memory, and are scarcely to be obtained. . . . Of our national nursery songs, some of them as old as our language, only a very common and inferior edition for children can be procured. Little Red Riding Hood and other tales hallowed to children's use, are now turned into ribaldry as satires for men. As for the creation of a new fairy tale or touching ballad, such a thing is unheard of. That the influence of all this is hurtful to children, the conductor of the proposed series firmly believes. He has practical experience of it every day in his own family, and he doubts not that there are many others who entertain the same opinion as himself. He purposes at least to give some evidence of his belief, and to produce a series of Works for children, the character of which may be briefly described as anti-Peter Parleyism.[19]

19. Lady Marian Fairman (Bond) Cole [Mrs. Felix Summerly], *The Mother's Primer: a Little Child's First Steps in Many Ways* (London, Longman, Brown,

All the books in the series were published by Cundall except *The Mother's Primer,* which was published in 1844 by Longman, Brown, Green, and Longmans. It was the only one in the series by Mrs. Felix Summerly (Lady Cole), who is thought of by modern educators as having been extremely enlightened. *The Mother's Primer* was printed in blue, red, and ochre in Caslon type, a face which had been discontinued about the beginning of the nineteenth century, but was revived by the Longman firm at the suggestion of Sir Henry Cole about 1845. *The Mother's Primer* of 1844 may be the earliest book to be printed by the Longman firm in this typeface. The geometric cover design of the Cundall books was redrawn and was also printed in the three colors. Henry Cole sent copies to the daughters of his close friend, William Makepeace Thackeray, who described them in an article in *Fraser's Magazine:* "The mere sight of the little books published by Mr. Cundall . . . is as good as a nosegay. Their actual colours are as brilliant as a bed of tulips, and blaze with emerald, and orange, and cobalt, and gold, and crimson. . . . Here are fairy tales, at last, with real pictures to them. What a library!—What a picture gallery."[20] The series included *Traditional Nursery Songs of England* offered to "all having charge of children, who are alive to the importance of cultivating their natural keeness for rhyme, rhythm, melody, and instinctive love of fun." It was published in 1843, the year after Halliwell-Phillips' *Nursery Rhymes of England* was published for the Percy Society.

Cole, who was knighted in 1875, was an influential man. He was instrumental in establishing the South Kensington Museum (which became the Victoria and Albert Museum) and he was largely responsible for the organization of the Great Exhibition of 1851. He became a close friend to the Prince Consort and proposed the building of the Royal Albert Hall as a memorial.

Cole's challenge for the creation of a modern fairy tale was answered by the Reverend Francis Edward Paget who in 1844 wrote *The Hope of the Katzekopfs: a Fairy Tale,* a book which later inspired Rudyard Kipling to write his *Rewards and Fairies.* In the preface, Paget wrote of "a desire to ascertain whether a race that has been glutted with Peter Parley, and Penny Magazines, and such like stories of (so called) useful knowledge, will condescend to read a Fable and its moral, or to interest them-

---

Green, and Longmans, 1844; reprinted by the Friends of the Osborne and Lillian H. Smith Collections, Toronto Public Library), 1970, p. 27.

20. William Makepeace Thackeray, "On Some Illustrated Children's Books" *Fraser's Magazine* 33:495-502 (April, 1846).

selves with the grotesque nonsense, the palpable, fantastic absurdities, the utter impossibilities of a Tale of Enchantment."[21] This book was published by James Burns, who the following year brought out *The Book of Nursery Tales.* A footnote recommends that "those who may be desirous of procuring these tales in a more illustrated and expensive form are recommended to Mr. F. Summerly's Home Library in which 'Beauty and the Beast', 'Little Red Riding-hood', and various others, appear in a large and handsome type, and with the addition of tinted or coloured plates."[22]

Cundall published simultaneously with the *Home Treasury* another series, *Gammer Gurton's Story Books,* edited by Ambrose Merton, the pseudonym of the scholar and librarian W. J. Thoms, who founded *Notes & Queries* in 1849 and also invented the word "folk-lore."

In 1846, the *Home Treasury* series was acquired by the firm of Chapman and Hall, who in February of that year brought out the first edition of the first English translation of Hans Christian Andersen's fairy tales, *Wonderful Stories,* translated by Mary Howitt. It preceded the Cundall edition, *A Danish Story-book,* translated by Charles Boner, by two weeks. Both books are in the Osborne Collection along with the Pickering edition of May, 1846.

The year 1846, in which Kate Greenaway and Randolph Caldecott were born, saw the publication of Edward Lear's *Book of Nonsense* and Richard Henry Horne's *Memoirs of a London Doll* (first published by Cundall and still in print). Frederick Marryat's *Children of the New Forest* was published in 1847. There is evidence that children during that time enjoyed these books of humor, imagination, and action. The Osborne Collection has several editions of Berquin's *Looking-glass for the Mind,* from the first E. Newbery edition of 1787 to the twentieth published in 1840. The "Advertisement" for the eighth edition of 1800 states that twenty thousand copies were sold during ten years. A girl named Mary Greaves, who had read one of the Osborne editions, heartily disliked the stories "where Virtue is constantly represented as the Fountain of Happiness and Vice as the Source of every Evil." She

21. Francis Edward Paget [William Churne, of Staffordshire], *The Hope of the Katzekopfs: a Fairy Tale* (Rugeley, John Thomas Walters; London, James Burns, 1844), p. xiv. (Reproduced in the series *Early Children's Books* sponsored by the Toronto Public Library and published by S. R. Publishers Ltd., and Johnson Reprint Corp., 1968.)

22. *The Book of Nursery Tales. A Keepsake for the Young* (London, James Burns, 1845), p. v.

changed the title-page from *The Looking-glass for the Mind, or Intellectual Mirror: Being an Elegant Collection of the Most Delightful Little Stories and Interesting Tales . . . With Seventy-four Cuts Designed and Engraved on Wood by I. Bewick,* to read: "The Looking-glass for the Mind, or *un*intellectual Mirror: being an *in*elegant collection of the most *disagreeable, silly* stories and *un*interesting tales . . . With twenty-four *ugly* cuts. Mary Greaves, age 13, 1849."[23]

Old John Harris died in November, 1846, leaving generous bequests to the Bookseller's Provident Retreat, to the Literary Fund, and the Printers' Pension Society. His son had sold the business in 1843 to Grant and Griffith, a partnership that continued until 1856 when the firm became Griffith and Farran. Grant and Griffith reprinted many of the old Harris titles from the "Cabinet of Amusement and Instruction." They published with Joseph Cundall a series called the *Favourite Library* which included Charles and Mary Lamb's *Mrs. Leicester's School,* first published by M. J. Godwin in 1809. They were joint publishers with Joseph Cundall in his *Treasury of Pleasure Books for Young Children* in 1850.

Cundall went into partnership with Addey, but this enterprise failed. He then published with, or designed and edited books for, other publishers such as Sampson Low, and David Bogue, who had followed Cundall as an assistant to Tilt and had succeeded to the firm on Tilt's retirement in 1842.

After 1850, books of adventure and fantasy written with well-defined plots and characterization came on the market and many of them are still being read by children today. Smith, Elder & Co. published Ruskin's *King of the Golden River* in 1851 and Thackeray's *Rose and the Ring* in 1855; John W. Parker, Printer to Cambridge University Press and publisher to the Society for Promoting Christian Knowledge, published Charlotte Yonge's *Little Duke* in 1854; the Macmillan firm published Kingsley's *Heroes* in 1856; and T. Nelson and Sons brought out Ballantyne's *Coral Island* in 1858.[24]

The firm of Dean & Son was very active during the 1850s, publishing innumerable series of toybooks: *Grandmamma Easy* and *Grandpapa Easy's Picture Books; Aunt Busy Bee's, Uncle Heart's Ease, Cousin Honeycomb's* and *Miss Merryheart's* series were a few of them. Many of

23. Arnaud Berquin, *The Looking-glass for the Mind . . .* 8th ed. (London, E. Newbery, 1800).

24. *Osborne Collection of Early Children's Books, a Catalogue,* 2 vols. (Toronto, Toronto Public Library, 1958-75).

Dean's toybooks were published in the United States by the McLoughlin firm. The Dean firm is still publishing in London today.

Darton & Co. of Holborn Hill was also active in the 1850s. In 1851 they published *The Exhibition* by F. W. N. Bayley in the *Little Folks' Laughing Library*, which was advertised as a "playful series . . . a humble attempt to elevate the juvenile literature of a land which is so finely and so holily devoted to its children."[25]

So many children's books were published in the 1850s that it is easy to understand why Houlston and Stoneman printed the following on the back cover of *Mamma's Budget:*

> It might at first sight appear almost presumptuous to suppose that there is yet room for an addition to our Juvenile Literature, but every person interested in the education of young people knows that the love of reading is an ever-increasing appetite, growing with what it feeds on, and that instructive and amusing books based on sound moral and Religious principles are never too numerous.[26]

Samuel Griswold Goodrich died in 1860. Near the end of his life he wrote:

> In looking at the long list of my publications, in reflecting upon the large numbers that have been sold, I feel far more of humiliation than of triumph . . . I have written too much, and have done nothing really well. You need not whisper it to the public, at least until I am gone; but I know, better than anyone can tell me, that there is nothing in this long catalogue that will give me a permanent place in literature.[27]

This confession is pathetic but it is true. Sir Henry Cole, who waged the battle against Peter Parleyism, lived until 1882 and was able to appreciate and enjoy the fruits of his campaign. He lived to see the publication of *Alice in Wonderland,* the books of George MacDonald, and Dinah Mulock's *Little Lame Prince.* In 1865, the year Frederick Warne, brother-in-law of George Routledge, set up his own business, George Routledge & Sons began to publish the toybooks illustrated by Walter Crane and printed by Edmund Evans, who had perfected the techniques of color printing. Cole lived to see the picture books of Randolph Caldecott and Kate Greenaway, published by the same firm. George Routledge,

25. Frederick William Naylor Bayley, *The Exhibition,* 2nd ed. (London, Darton and Co., 1851), The Little folks' laughing library, back cover.

26. *Mamma's Budget: or Daily Reading for Little Children,* 3rd ed. (London, Houlston & Stoneman, 1854), back cover.

27. Goodrich, *Recollections,* vol. II, pp. 333-34.

the founder, boasted on his retirement in 1880 that during his long career he had published five thousand books, an average of two a week.

Dame Marian Cole, who died in 1892, lived to see the colored fairy books of Andrew Lang and Robert Louis Stevenson's *Child's Garden of Verses,* all published by Longmans, Green and Co. Perhaps it was Lady Cole who inspired her husband to publish the *Home Treasury* series that heralded this Golden Age of Children's Literature, an age that we in the 1970s have reason to envy. It is fortunate for the children of today that publishers are wisely keeping in print many excellent books of the nineteenth century which continue to cultivate the "imagination and taste" of the rising generation.

Books in Parts and the Number Trade

Mihai H. Handrea

Mihai H. Handrea is the Librarian of the Carl H. Pforzheimer Library in New York City.

"To Booksellers and Stationers: a person in the above line of business wishes to accept a commission to travel, or to be engaged in a warehouse. Security will be given if required. . . ." This situation-wanted ad was inserted in the October issue, 1827, of the *Monthly Literary Advertiser,* later to be known as *Bent's Literary Advertiser,* under the heading "Literary Intelligence." The paper was published in London on the tenth of every month and out-of-town copies were sent post-free. Its eight pages carried publishers' announcements in several categories: works now first published, lately published, new editions, fine arts, odds and ends of literary information, works preparing for publication, and to these was added a list of new books which had been published in the previous month.

The least costly advertisement in this paper was seven shillings for eight lines of a column of text. At least one of the papers allowed a reduction for situation-wanted ads which could be placed for only five shillings.[1] Though this amount represented a full day's wages for some, it was not too expensive an investment if it could lead to lucrative employment. Here is another advertisement from the March, 1829, issue of the same paper: "A young man who has travelled during the last 8

---

1. As quoted in *Bell's Weekly Messenger,* 7 September 1823, about advertising in the *Morning Chronicle.*

years for a house of the first respectability in the book trade . . . looks for a situation as traveller or clerk."

These travelers were known as canvassers. In terms of respectability, their calling was one rung above that of hawkers of chapbooks and ballad sheets at country fairs and in market places. They were door-to-door salesmen of books issued piecemeal over a period of time, offered to the public in weekly numbers or in monthly parts, and sold by the unit at a fraction of the cost of the entire book. Selling in installments was making reading matter accessible to a wide range of the population who otherwise could not afford the purchase of a book.

The system was known as the "number trade": it was a form of bookselling prevalent in the provinces, particularly in the North and Midlands, based on personal contact with a prospective customer. Though number books had begun appearing as early as the last quarter of the seventeenth century,[2] the system of book distribution through canvassers came into its own by the middle of the second decade of the nineteenth century and flourished particularly in the 1820s. Contributing to its widespread practice were economic, social, technological, and cultural conditions which will be discussed later.

Charles Knight, writing about a category of part and number books circulated in this fashion, suggests, with some exaggeration, that successful sales depended not so much on the quality of the merchandise as on the charisma of the itinerant salesman:

> The system upon which they are sold is essentially that of forcing a sale; and the necessary cost of this forcing, called 'canvassing', is sought to be saved in the quantity of the article 'canvassed', . . . The 'canvasser' is an universal genius, and must be paid as men of genius ought to be paid. He has to force off the commonest of wares by the most ingenious of devices. It is not the intrinsic merit of a book that is to command a sale, but the exterior accomplishments of the salesman. He adapts himself to every condition of person with whom he is thrown into contact. As in Birmingham and other great towns there is a beggars' register, which describes the susceptibilities of the families at whose gates beggars call, even to the particular theological opinions of the occupants, so the canvasser has a pretty accurate account of the households within his boat. He knows where there is a customer in the kitchen, and the customer in the parlour. He sometimes has a timid colloquy with the cook in the passage; sometimes takes a glass of ale in the servants' hall; and,

2. R. M. Wiles, *Serial Publication in England before 1750* (Cambridge: The University Press, 1957), p. 270.

when he can rely upon the charms of his address, sends his card boldly into the drawing-room. No refusal can prevent him in the end leaving his number for inspection. . . .[3]

I have made various attempts to trace a "beggars' register" and see for myself the kind of information which would have enabled the itinerant seller of books in parts to ply his trade successfully, but to no avail. No doubt one must exist.

I have come to the conclusion, however, that in a great many instances what the canvassers used were local directories or "strangers' guides," well established by the early part of the nineteenth century, and used by a variety of commercial travelers.

All the conditions which had made directories generally acceptable—improved communications, development of industry, spread of home and foreign trade, growing size of population and its increasing concentration in towns—continued with redoubled force as the century went on . . . coaches halved the time taken between London and the north and speeded up travel between the principal towns. Producers sought for markets over ever-wider areas, and at the same time trade sprang up in remote places which had hardly known it before.[4]

Before the 1830s separate lists of private addresses were already beginning to appear in provincial directories. *Gore's Liverpool Directory* for 1803 had the names, addresses, and occupations of town and surrounding country residents listed in the main alphabet. Among them are found upholsterers, schoolmasters, liquor dealers, musicians and music sellers, dancing masters, attorneys, hair dressers, grocers, shopkeepers, and many others, while special groups such as the clergy, bankers, and local members of parliament were included under special headings. There is detailed information, for instance, in Edward Baines's *History, Directory & Gazetteer of the County of York*, 1822–1823, with an index of places and population returns, and with alphabetical classifications for professional and trade categories. The directory excludes only laborers and those persons connected with trades arising from the sale of their own produce. Information on private citizens as "householders of respectability" was made available in some provincial directories—as in the case of Liverpool and its vicinity—by 1827, and special directories such

3. Charles Knight, *The Old Printer and the Modern Press* (London: John Murray, 1854), p. 216-17.
4. Jane E. Norton, *Guide to the National and Provincial Directories of England and Wales* . . . (London: Offices of The Royal Historical Society, 1950), p. 9.

as the one issued by Isaac Cottrill of Newcastle-under-Lyme listed local householders with their occupations and residences.

These provincial directories were available in various places along a canvasser's route such as local coffee houses, police stations, newspaper offices, and booksellers' shops. The booksellers themselves must have provided by word of mouth valuable information on the "susceptibilities" of the local residents to the particular types of number and part books which would be most saleable in the community. The practice is amply demonstrated in an account of a traveling salesman in 1830 who covered fourteen hundred miles in three months, by foot, by coach, and by gig, pushing the serial publication of an edition of the *Encyclopaedia Britannica.*[5] Gypsies and road tramps used cabalistic signs known to their own fraternity to indicate residences where an appeal to hospitality would be likely to meet with success, as well as the "dead hard marks," the places where no beggar ever called.[6] The "beggars' registers" mentioned earlier were, no doubt, a combination of useful knowledge derived from some or all of these sources.[7]

The canvasser's "card," announcing the purpose of one's call at a particular stop, was frequently a prospectus of a work to be published, or then being published in parts, issued by the proprietor. One such example is a three-by-five-inch, six-page leaflet printed by William Clowes and used as a prospectus and specimen for *The Modern Traveller,* a work published in monthly parts at two shillings sixpence each by James Duncan of London, 1827.[8] The leaflet lists the terms of publication: how many sheets of letter-press, how many plates and maps, the type used, and so on. One could gather that *The Modern Traveller* was in the course of publication because of excerpts from notices in *Blackwood's Magazine,* the *Literary Gazette,* and the *New Monthly Magazine* extolling the work for its accuracy and appearance. Often during his

5. James Cannon, ed., "'On the Road' One Hundred Years Ago: a Trade Journey in 1830," in *The Publishers' Circular and the Publisher & Bookseller,* Feb. 9–April 13, 1935.

6. Jim Phelan, *We Follow the Roads* (London: Phoenix House, 1949), p. 99. I am indebted for this suggestion to Dorothy McCulla, Librarian of the Local Studies Department, Birmingham Public Libraries.

7. There is mention of an annotated directory used by a commercial traveler in a different branch of trade in Norton's *Guide,* p. 9.

8. In the Arents Collection of Books in Parts, New York Public Library. I wish to record here my appreciation for the courtesy and assistance received during my research on this paper from the staff of the Arents Collection: Jeffrey Kaimowitz, Bernard McTigue, and Joseph Rankin, curator.

calls at the shops of provincial booksellers, newspaper offices, and else-where, the traveler for the *Encyclopaedia Britannica* in 1830 left similar leaflets to be distributed among the local citizenry.

Another customary means of advertising titles in stock through the network of canvassers was a catalog. Let us consider one example: *Catalogue, for 1832, of Useful Standard Works, Published by Mackenzie & Dent, Newcastle upon Tyne, and Sold by Mr. James Arthur, Carlisle; Mr. James Fenton, Alnwick; Mr. P. Grant, Berwick; and Mr. D. Mackenzie, Glasgow.*[9] This is a four-page octavo leaflet, roughly eight-and-a-half by five-and-a-half inches, divided into three parts: "Works in General Literature, Arts, Sciences, &c.," "Works on Divinity and Morality," and "Works of Amusement and Genius," with twenty-six titles listed in the first category, twenty-two in the second, and thirty-six in the last, or a total of eighty-four books to be purchased on the installment plan, the only exception advertised being *Johnson's Pocket Dictionary of the English Language* for three shillings sixpence bound in sheep and embellished with a beautiful portrait. Of these eighty-four titles, only four are directly identified as being publications issued by Eneas Mackenzie I in partnership with John Moore Dent: a topographical work on Durham sold at one shilling a number; *Choice Biography* in thirty-two numbers; and *Mackenzie's Complete System of Modern Geography* in one hundred ten numbers, each at sixpence a number.

In ten cases, the work listed is currently being published and the length is given only as "in about" so many numbers, or "to be completed" in so many numbers. In a few instances, a particular title is available both in numbers and in parts, such as *The Artists & Mechanics' Encyclopaedia* in eighty quarto numbers at sixpence each or in parts at five shillings each, or *Lawson's Modern Farrier* in twenty-six numbers or in four parts. One other work listed this way is a *History of Northumberland,* subdivided into forty-two and one-half quarto numbers at one shilling each, or eight-and-a-half parts at five shillings each. All other books are

9. A copy of the catalog in the Bell Collection was made available to me by the staff of the Newcastle Public Library and I am grateful to them for their courteous assistance. C. J. Hunt, *The Book Trade in Northumberland and Durham to 1860* (Newcastle upon Tyne, 1975), offers information on Eneas Mackenzie I and John Moore Dent, the partners in the firm but omits listing James Fenton and P. Grant although both were engaged in the book trade in the area. As for James Arthur of Carlisle, Cumberland, the traveler for the *Encyclopaedia Britannica* in 1830, comments that he is "a NO man whose punctuality of payment is not much to be depended on. Would give specimens to his canvassers to show about the country."

offered at the going rate of sixpence a number. Most, if not all, of the titles in the catalog are descriptive of the work and serve as "publicity plugs." A few examples are in order.

From "Works in General Literature, Arts, Sciences, &c.":

THE YOUNG WOMAN'S GUIDE

To Virtue, Economy, and Happiness, containing a complete and elegant System of Domestic Cookery, formed upon Principles of Economy; and other Subjects essential to the Attainment of every domestic, elegant, and intellectual Accomplishment; with 12 Engravings. In 25 Numbers, at 6 pence each.

ROSINA;
OR, THE VIRTUOUS COUNTRY MAID

Being Memoirs of the Marchioness of Lemington. Written by herself, to instruct her own Sex by shewing the Dangers attending extraordinary Beauty in Females of humble Rank, and the Security and Happiness imparted by Virture. Embellished by numerous Engravings. In 26 Numbers, at 6 pence each.

From "Works on Divinity and Morality":

SELECT MEMOIRS

Of the Lives, Labours, and Sufferings of those pious and learned ENGLISH AND SCOTTISH DIVINES, who greatly distinguished themselves in promoting the Reformation from Popery, in translating the Bible, and in promulgating its salutary Doctrines by their numerous Evangelical Writings. Introduced with an historical Sketch of the Christian Church. By Thomas Smith. In about 26 Numbers, at 6 pence each.

WESLEY'S HYMNS,

For the Use of the People called Methodists. In 12 Nos. 6 pence each, with a Head of the Author.

Part III, "Works of Amusement and Genius," consists mostly of fiction and reads like a roll call of titles from Montague Summers's *A Gothic Bibliography*.

A notice preceding the lists spells out the procedure by which customers were reached:

A Perusal of this Catalogue is requested, as the Bearer will call again, when Specimens of the different Works may be seen, and Subscriptions received. The numbers, which will be regularly delivered, one or two at a time, as may suit the Convenience of the Purchaser, are to be paid for on delivery.—To prevent imperfect Sets, Subscribers must continue till the end of the Work. The Publishers pledge themselves to complete their respective Works.

Some of the canvassers were given stock on credit and were expected to settle the accounts periodically in return for a previously agreed-upon remuneration which was usually regulated by the volume of sales.[10] Others, who were well established in their respective territories, purchased outright a quantity of stock at a discount and disposed of it for their own benefit.[11]

Only a few titles in the Mackenzie and Dent catalog were identified as their own publications. Going through the advertising pages of contemporary London and provincial papers, sifting through lists of number and part works printed on the wrappers of some of the titles in the catalog, and checking clues elsewhere, about half of the titles could be traced to two publishers: twenty-four titles to George Virtue and eighteen titles to Thomas Kelly, the leaders of the "number trade" at the time.[12]

The Virtue and Kelly publications are represented, respectively, by three titles and six titles in "Works in General Literature, Arts, Sciences, &c."; three and ten under "Works on Divinity and Morality"; and eighteen and two titles under "Works of Amusement and Genius."

In effect, Mackenzie & Dent of Newcastle upon Tyne were acting as agents to the two London giants of the "number trade." To its own printing, publishing, and bookselling business, Mackenzie & Dent, like many other firms in the provinces, had added the job of marketing the product of out-of-town publishers through its network of canvassers.

Among the novelists whose "numbered" works are offered by the

10. A similar method was employed by George Miller of Haddington and Dunbar, Scotland. See his *Latter Struggles in the Journey of Life* . . . (Edinburgh: Printed by James Colston for the Author, 1833), p. 147 and following.

11. Joseph Ogle Robinson of Hurst, Robinson, and Co., in a letter to Archibald Constable, from London, 11 July 1825, on the type of profits to be derived from number-publishing: "You may perhaps gather some ideas from the following statement:—Stevens published the History of the Wars of the French Revolution in two vols. quarto, and it died almost as soon as it appeared, and some years after it was made into wastepaper. Baines of Leeds republished it . . . and circulated through the hawkers above 20,000 copies in 6d. Nos.; but, if my memory is correct, Davies and Booth and other great hawkers only paid Baines 2½ d. per No. When I was at Leeds, . . . I saw much of the concerns of Davies and Booth, who were the greatest people in this line out of London, and they generally considered that 2d. was as much as they could afford for 6d. Nos., but on account of the popularity of Baines's book they gave him 2½ d." Thomas Constable, *Archibald Constable and his Literary Correspondents* (Edinburgh: Edmonston and Douglas, 1873), iii, p. 364.

12. For an account of these two publishers, see the chapter, "Kelly and Virtue: the 'Number Trade'," in Henry Curwen's *A History of Booksellers, the Old and the New* (London: Chatto and Windus, 1873), p. 363-78. See also Richard Cramp-

Mackenzie & Dent catalog are found, not unexpectedly, some of the Minerva Press authors, such as Mrs. Ward, Elizabeth Helme, Maria Regina Roche, and Francis Lathom. There are eight titles on the list by Catharine George Ward, afterwards Mrs. Mason, of which at least seven had been published by Virtue in the previous decade, the dates ranging from 1821—*The Mysterious Marriage*—to 1827, *The Fisher's Daughter* and *The Knight of the White Banner*. Of Elizabeth Helme's two titles, *The Farmer of Inglewood Forest* and *St. Clair's of the Isles,* issued by Virtue about 1825, the former was published by the Minerva Press as early as 1796. Francis Lathom's *The Mysterious Freebooter* first came out as a Minerva Press production in 1806. Mrs. Roche's *Children of the Abbey,* another enduring success of popular literature, was published in 1796. Of the nine Hannah Maria Jones titles listed in Montague Summers up to the year 1831, five appear in the Mackenzie & Dent catalog, all issued by Virtue between 1824 and 1831.

In some cases, Virtue had also issued these works as bound volumes. Mrs. Ward's *The Mysterious Marriage* was offered to the public in September of 1824 as a duodecimo four-volume set at twenty-one shillings and Mary Leman Grimstone's *Louisa Egerton* as a three-decker in May of 1830 at twenty-one shillings.

Note that these same two works, offered in numbers and purchased individually, cost a lot less than the bound editions: Ward's *The Mysterious Marriage* in twenty-seven numbers at sixpence each, and Grimstone's *Louisa Egerton* in twenty-four numbers, also sixpence, come to only thirteen-and-a-half and twelve shillings respectively. This, by the way, did not always hold true, and books purchased by the number could run to expensive totals. Of course, the advantage of acquiring the book by the piece remained attractive since the expense could be divided into small regular sums more easily afforded by the poor.

Of the other titles in the Mackenzie & Dent catalog which can be traced to George Virtue number publications, at least two are eighteenth-century works and represent instances of expired copyrights. The same is true of the works issued by Thomas Kelly, but in a larger measure. The catalog also includes some bibles, devotional treatises, works on topography and biography, the natural sciences, home and horse medicine, self-improvement aimed at both sexes, history, legal practice, cooking, music, and, above all, reprints of popular fiction then much in demand.

---

ton's Fell's *Passages from the Private and Official Life of . . . Alderman Kelly . . .* (London, 1856).

There do not seem to be any "first editions" on the list. As a matter of fact, part of the puffery which was intended to increase the prospective buyer's interest was the practice of continually announcing "new" editions as evidence of the work's long-lasting popularity. On the back wrapper of Number 6 of *The Victim of Fashion* by Hannah Maria Jones, a list of "new & entertaining works, now publishing in numbers and parts" under the name of George Virtue includes Mrs. Ward's *The Mysterious Marriage* in its twelfth edition. The date is 1824; Mrs. Ward's book is listed as available complete either in seven parts at two shillings each or in twenty-seven numbers at sixpence each. The Mackenzie & Dent catalog of 1832 lists the work as being available in twenty-seven numbers at the going rate of sixpence the number. To the 1824 part and number formats of this particular title, can also be added the four volume set.

I have traced some of George Virtue's number publications in the Mackenzie & Dent catalog in order to see how some of them were put together. The one selected for discussion herein will demonstrate a few facts about publication makeup.

Let us look at *The Victim of Fashion* by Hannah Maria Jones. The copy in the Arents Collection of Books in Parts was issued in twenty-eight numbers bound in twenty-four, numbers 21-22, 23-24, 25-26, and 27-28 being double numbers. Arabic numerals are stamped in the upper left corner of the printed wrappers. Eight of the wrappers are light brown in color, two of them on a different stock in a darker shade; the rest light tan. The setting of the front wrappers is the same throughout; there are four settings of the back wrappers. Eighteen of the back wrappers, including the first and the last ones, have G. Virtue's advertisement and prospects for *Oxberry's Dramatic Biography,* another title in the Mackenzie & Dent catalog.[13]

Each single number is made up of twenty-four pages, or three half-sheets of an octavo, side-stitched through the wrappers. The pagination is continuous, the text ending on page 672. The printed title page, present here in Number 1, is included in the pagination.

The wrapper title reads *The Victim of Fashion, or The Gamblers, Founded on Recent Facts.* The price is sixpence throughout, even for the

---

13. According to the Lowe-Arnott-Robinson *English Theatrical Literature 1559-1900* (London: The Society for Theatre Research, 1970), n. 4139, it began appearing on 1 January 1825. Thus, the original numbers did constitute a "first edition," it is unlikely, however, that the copies distributed years later in 1832 through the Mackenzie & Dent firm were part of that first printing.

double numbers of forty-eight pages each. To the right of the price is the heading "Virtue's New Works."

Also on the front wrapper is a capsule description of what is being offered: ". . . the most delightfully entertaining Work that has for a length of time engaged the attention of the Public; for its moral is impressive, and its scenes, though seductive, are not dangerous, because 'Vice is certainly a monster of such frightful mien, that to be hated needs only to be seen'; . . ."[14]

At the bottom of the back wrappers, as printer, is the name of C[harles]. Baynes, 13, Duke Street, Lincoln's Inn Fields. The frequency of publication, whether weekly or fortnightly, is not stated, but a promise is added: "To be completed in about 24 numbers price 6 pence each, and embellished with an elegant frontispiece and other appropriate engravings, by the first artist." The wrappers are dated 1824.

Two engraved portraits and seven plates are issued with numbers 1, 3, 6, 9, 12, 15, 18, 21-22, and 25-26, all save two published by Virtue. In the frontispiece position is inserted a plate depicting a dramatic scene, with the caption "Cecilia screamed but the fatal trigger was drawn, and he fell a lifeless corpse at her feet." Engraved on each plate is the number of the page to which it refers. The two other plates bear the name of E[dwin]. Livermore, Albion Press, 50 Fetter Lane, as publisher. Livermore's name also appears as a colophon twice, on verso of the printed title leaf and after the text: E. Livermore, Printer, 119 Fleet Street.[15] The printed title differs from the one on the front wrappers: *The Victim of Fashion; or, A Treacherous Friend,* and the date is 1825.

The running head in the first number is "The victim of fashion, or" on versos, and "The gamblers" on rectos, but with Number 2 it changes to "The gamblers" on both sides and so it remains to the end.

Last but not least, one particular element missing here, which is present in all other number or part books issued by George Virtue in the 1820s and printed by Charles Baynes, is the numerals, usually printed in the lower left corner of the first leaf of each of the three octavo half-sheets making up a published section of a book. For instance, the Number 2 of a given title would have each of its three four-leaf gatherings,

14. A somewhat loose quotation from Alexander Pope's *An Essay on Man,* Epistle II, lines 217-18.

15. Not listed at this address in William B. Todd's *A Directory of Printers . . .* or in Pigot's *Directory* 1824 either at this address or at 50 Fetter Lane. The latter address is given as the place of business for T. Howard, glass and Staffordshire china warehouseman.

B, C, and D, also marked with that number, in this case a "2" printed in the lower left corner of the rectos of B1, C1, and D1. At least in one case I have seen, the internal marking of half sheets which identifies their position in numerical sequence is further refined and appears thus: *a*2 on D, *b*2 on E, *c*2 on F, placing them in proper order for collating the Number 2 of that title.

It was customary, though by no means universal practice, for the printed title page and other front matter to be included in the last published number or part, the text usually beginning with signature B. The year of publication, as printed on the title page, was usually that of the last published part or number, although the first part or number may have been published in an earlier year. When plates were issued, it was customary to print instructions to the binder in the last number or part giving their position in the text. It also was customary, on an occasion when a number work had been promised in so many units, that all extra numbers were given free to subscribers. This, apparently, was the case here, the work being announced "in about 24 nos." but completed in twenty-eight.

That two printers' names appear, Charles Baynes's on the wrappers and Edwin Livermore's in the colophon, points to one of two facts. Either the wrappers were printed in a different shop from that in which the letterpress work was done, or wrappers and letterpress belonged to two distinct printings of the book. The situation is further complicated by the mixed plates, some published by Livermore and some by Virtue, and by the change in the running head. Probably the copy in the Arents Collection of Books in Parts was made up of remainder sheets used for all numbers after the first when the running head changes to "The gamblers," and the set was undoubtedly put together in a warehouse where plates published by Livermore and Virtue were currently available. There is an edition listed in the British Library catalog as *The Gamblers; or, The Treacherous Friend; a Moral Tale, Founded on Recent Facts, By the Author of Several Popular Works, Embellished with Engravings,* in octavo, of six hundred seventy-two pages, and with the imprint "E. Livermore: London, 1824." I have not seen a copy and therefore cannot say for certain that it, too, appeared in numbers; but by dividing six hundred seventy-two by twenty-four, the result is twenty-eight, the number of units in which the work was eventually published.

Even for a half-educated guess at the bibliographical makeup of a set of numbers, several unsophisticated sets of the same work would be needed, ideally sets that could be traced to the same vendor and purchaser, or some other information from a warehouse ledger, as well as much else. I have seen, on occasion, a complete set of numbers bearing the name of a former owner, but I could not vouch whether the numbers had been purchased from the same bookseller, one at a time, or a few at a time immediately upon publication, or at a later date. In some sets I have looked at, a bookseller's label is sometimes pasted onto the wrappers of a few of the numbers, but never for an entire set.

The Mackenzie & Dent catalog was typical of its times. What it offered to a new and growing reading public was a balanced diet of reading matter consisting mostly of so-called "cheap literature," selling at twopence a half sheet, with an occasional engraving or woodcut thrown in as an added attraction. When the nature of the work called for a greater number of plates, such as *The History of Northumberland,* "each with fine engravings," the price of the numbers increases correspondingly to one shilling and that of a part, to five. But only a few of these were listed, because the catalog was aimed at a category of the reading public which publishers had been slow in recognizing before. It excluded, naturally, the part and number works which, even in serial production, were expensive, such as *The History and Antiquities of the Tower of London* at three pound thirteen shillings and sixpence a part, or Audubon's *Birds* in double elephant folio at two pounds two shillings a part. These kinds of works were called in the trade "furniture books" or "companions of the drawing-room," the counterparts of today's coffee-table publications.

Not surprisingly then, when number or part books were advertised in the papers, they were almost, without exception, the expensive kind which appealed to elite buyers, who could afford a guinea and a half for the latest three-decker novel or the exorbitant sum of thirty pounds for the sumptuously produced *Original Works of Hogarth* in 24 numbers. Advertising in the papers was expensive—the taxes on knowledge, amounting to three shillings and sixpence for a single entry, was passed on to the buyer of advertising space with the result that publicity for the book trade was costly. Only the established firms could afford to advertise regularly. By the nature of their subject matter and by the method of their distribution, the Mackenzie & Dent catalog number and part books were directed at a special market with special needs, but with limited means to satisfy these needs.

The year 1832 is significant in this respect. It marked a midway point in a series of developments that encouraged the expansion of the "number" book trade while providing the "industrious classes" with an easy means to satisfy their reading needs with periodic small investments in knowledge. Indeed, entire books have been written on the economic, social, technological, and cultural background against which the English common reader emerges during the first three or four decades of the nineteenth century. Only the barest outline of some of these conditions and trends will be sketched here.

The spread of education which created an ever-increasing demand for reading matter was the result of the interplay of conflicting entities. The religious force first sought to replace the much maligned peddlers' chapbooks and ballad sheets at the end of the eighteenth century with the Cheap Repository Tracts which disguised their moralizing purpose under the appearance of penny books. The established classes—alarmed at finding out that the lower orders had been stirred up by the radical ferment of the French Revolution—tried to replace the "twopenny trash" periodicals and political pamphlets of social reformers with suitably inoffensive reading matter.

Schools of every denomination mushroomed after 1780. One group alone, the National Society for Educating the Poor according to the Principles of the Established Church, could boast by 1830 of 3,670 schools with an enrollment of 346,000 pupils. By the 1830s, between two-thirds and three-quarters of the English working classes could read.[16]

As larger numbers of people learned to read, the need for cheap and politically safe reading matter grew larger. Until 1827, when the so-called cheap "libraries" (*Constable's Miscellany,* the *Library of Useful Knowledge,* and other series after them) began to appear, increases in book prices placed publications of copyright works out of the common people's reach. Even the price of five or six shillings for a volume of so-called cheap literature was expensive considering that it often represented a full day's wages. Established lending libraries in the populated urban areas, such as the Minerva Public Library of Leadenhall Street, London, had rates which made them accessible to the carriage trade only. In the provinces, there were many fly-by-night small lending libraries of tattered tomes which often changed hands and location, but their contents were often made up of the same reprints which appeared in number trade catalogs. Therefore, buying a book in installments was not only much easier on the pocket but added the pride of possession to the pleasure of reading.

Better communications between various towns made easier the dis-

16. R. K. Webb, *The British Working Class Reader 1790-1848: Literacy and Social Tension* (London: George Allen & Unwin, 1955), p. 17, 22.

tribution of part and number publications through local booksellers, newsagents, and canvassers. Technological advances in the production of books—such as the perfecting of the plaster-of-Paris method of making stereotypes, the Fourdriniers' paper-making machine, the use of steam in printing—were successfully applied to serial publication by 1832, the year of the Mackenzie & Dent catalog. During this same year *Chambers' Journal* and the *Penny Magazine* began, to be followed by the *Penny Cyclopaedia* and a few other inexpensive periodical publications.

The new and growing reading public was by now quite used to spending sixpence a week, or a few pennies at a time to purchase reading matter. In fact, these readers, whose taste became better educated, and who expected good as well as cheap literature, were quite prepared to spend a shilling a month to buy exciting new fiction. At the same time, publishers were prepared to acknowledge and fulfill their needs.

While it is true that the number trade expansion was motivated by gain and that it deliberately created its own market, it was no less true that it provided reading matter for people which they could afford. Thus, the number trade was a force which helped establish reading habits and contributed to people's enlightenment.

It may seem that the reading matter provided by the number trade was far from exciting. However, what held great appeal to many common readers was a special genre of "real life romance," particularly the kind which would relate the facts and circumstances connected with a sensational crime and which publishers in the number trade were usually quick to turn out.

A case in point will permit us to look at the other side of Thomas Kelly's publishing activities. Thomas Kelly, who rose from rags to riches and who eventually became Lord Mayor of London, was a giant of the number trade who came to be remembered for having sold 250,000 copies of 12 separate editions of the Bible, 100,000 copies of *The Life of Christ,* and 20,000 copies of *The History of the French Revolution.*[17] His detractors accused him of never investing any money in the production of new works. He was more interested, they claimed, in opening up new territories for his canvassers and in pushing the sale of countless reprints of books out of copyright, than in encouraging the publication of original literature.

This was not true. After Princess Charlotte, daughter of the Regent, died during childbirth in 1817, Kelly published in six monthly parts a

17. Figures quoted from Curwen, *A History of Booksellers,* p. 370.

phenomenally successful *Memoirs* . . . , compiled by Robert Huish, a prolific miscellaneous writer called by some an "obscure and unscrupulous scribbler."[18] Encouraged by a sale of 50,000 copies, Kelly reissued the work in numbers, in 1818–19, using the same plates. In 1830, on the death of Charlotte's father, by this time George IV, Kelly once again commissioned Robert Huish to compile for serial publication the late monarch's *Memoirs* in twelve monthly parts, and it also was highly successful. Yet one of Kelly's most successful productions in numbers and parts centered on a sensational murder trial which came to be known as the "Murder in the Red Barn.[19]

The owner of the barn in the vicinity of Polstead, Suffolk, was a rich young farmer by the name of William Corder, who had been living in sin with the daughter of a mole-catcher, Maria Marten. She nagged and threatened him that he should make an honest woman of her until, at long last, Corder pretended to comply and proposed a secret marriage. Maria left her parents' cottage on the night of May 18, 1827. Corder met her in the fields, lured her into the barn on his property, killed her, stuffed her corpse into a sack, buried her in a makeshift grave, and later had the barn filled with grain. For a while, he dodged her family's inquiries as to Maria's whereabouts by telling them that they had been united in holy matrimony and that she was living in another town until he felt he could break the news of his misalliance to his parents. Then, he left for London, where he advertised in the papers for a wife, eventually married a governess, and with her opened a girls' school at Brentford. Meanwhile Maria's mother had been dreaming dreams from which she apprehended that Corder had destroyed her daughter and had buried her in the Red Barn. At last, her husband went to look. Almost a year later, Maria's remains were found. Corder was arrested, tried at Bury Assizes, and hanged before an enormous crowd on the morning of August 11, 1828.

No sooner did the news break out, than the papers began to make the most of the story. The *Weekly Dispatch* distributed on April 20 a handbill announcing that the next number would contain a full account of the murder, advising its potential audience that all postmasters and newsagents would take orders for the special issue which, as was customary, would be delivered postage free within a radius of 120 miles from Lon-

18. Montague Summers, *A Gothic Bibliography* (London, Fortune Press [1940]), p. 71. Huish also produced on order for Thomas Kelly books on George III and Queen Caroline.

19. *The Annual Register . . . of the Year 1828*, p. 106-7, p. 337-49.

don.[20] A local printer, S. Piper of Ipswich, beat the *Weekly Dispatch* by a day, and published a penny broadsheet in black mourning border on April 26, "Discovery of a Horrid Murder at Polstead, Suffolk." Almost immediately the firm of Knight and Lacey, booksellers at 55 Paternoster Row, started publishing a fictionalized account of the event under the catchy title of *The Red Barn; a Tale Founded on Facts,* in sixpenny weekly numbers.

Thomas Kelly, realizing a good opportunity when he came upon one, took some time in organizing his plans: while Knight and Lacey were providing the number trade market with "a tale founded on facts," Kelly commissioned J. Curtis, a shorthand reporter for the *Times,* to do leg-work for him at the scene of the crime. J. Curtis left London on St. Swithin's Day, July 15, for Suffolk. By then the preliminary inquest had implicated Corder and his guilt was confirmed at a trial a few weeks later.

Once he had his own man on the spot, Kelly publicized his venture. A handbill was issued announcing publication of Number One, price six-pence, of *An Authentic and Faithful History of the Mysterious Murder of Maria Marten in the Red Barn,* . . . taken in short hand by a gentleman specially retained for this edition. . . ." Kelly's agents and various book-sellers circulated the bill throughout the country. An advertisement was inserted in a local paper naming six agents—four in Suffolk, and two in nearby Essex—who sold the sixpenny numbers.[21] At the time of the trial, August 7 and 8, a 15-x-10-inch broadsheet was printed in Kelly's name with "now publishing" news of his edition.

The work appeared in twenty-four numbers, dressed in attractively printed mustard yellow wrappers. Beginning with No. 11, the front wrap-per stated that the work was also available in parts at two shillings each.

There is some evidence that Kelly tried to rush his edition onto the market. I quote from his advertisement printed on the back wrappers: "The Work will be published in Numbers, *in as quick succession as cir-cumstances will permit* [emphasis added]. When completed, it will form one of the most interesting volumes that can be placed in the hands of young or old, an authentic detail of the awful consequences that have been produced by an early departure from a course of virtue, piety, and uprightness, as has been the case with the unhappy subjects of this Narrative."

20. This handbill, together with other ephemera connected with the case, is mounted in a scrapbook in the Arents Collection of Books in Parts.

21. The agents were J. Dingle, Bury; W. Driver, Boxford; J. Danzie, North Street, Sudbury; C. A. Pask, Ipswich—all of Suffolk—and I. Hogg, Colchester, and E. Sutton, Chelmsford, both of Essex.

Some collating irregularities in the first three numbers are further evidence that the job was done in haste. Thereafter, the amount of letterpress alternates from three to two half sheets of an octavo per issue, two half sheets being worked together at the same time. William Clowes was the printer.

The earliest date found on a plate is August 2, the latest October 11, 1828, both Saturdays. The copy of Kelly's edition that I have seen in the Arents Collection has lost the stitches which usually keep wrappers and contents together. While the plates are inserted in the right places in the text, their dates do not follow one another, proving they were not issued in chronological order. It also seems that the demand must occasionally have surpassed the supply, for two of the numbers are covered in plain brown wrappers, stamped in ink inside and out with their respective serial position and the word "Polstead."

While Thomas Kelly was publishing his numbers, other publishers did not remain idle. A locally printed broadsheet was sold at one penny each on the second day of the trial, August 8.[22] On August 10, after Corder had been sentenced, the *Weekly Dispatch* presented "Gratis to the Readers," a portrait of the criminal below a sketch of the Red Barn. The same day, the papers published Corder's confession, and a Bury bookseller flooded the town with the traditional "A Copy of Verses Written by William Corder, whilst under Sentence of Death in the Condemned Cell, for ᵗʰe Murder of Maria Marten."[23] Jemmy Catnach's broadsheets had alreaᵈy appeared, to be followed by one published by Birt, from his song and ballad warehouse in the Seven Dials district.[24] Another local bookseller turned publisher for the occasion, T. C. Newby of Bury, announced on August 12 the publication at sixpence of a sensational sheet, *The Confession, the Last Words, Execution and Dissection of Corder,* while the *Weekly Dispatch* of the first Sunday after the hanging "presented gratuitously to the purchasers" of the paper a so-called correct view of the event, with the head of Corder "as it appeared on the dissecting table."

Corder's Love Letters Sent by Nearly One Hundred Ladies in Answer

22. The work of J. Raw, Printer, Ipswich.
23. "Printed by J. Robinson, Bookseller, Bookbinder and Stationer, Traverse, Bury; where may be had Dutton's and Newby's editions of the trial of William Corder."
24. *Particulars of the Trial & Execution of William Corder Who Was Executed at Bury St. Edmunds, on Monday, August 11, 1828, for the Wilful Murder of Maria Marten* (London: Thomas Birt, 1828).

to his Matrimonial Advertisement was sold at four pence,[25] Knight and Lacey published an appendix to their edition in six more numbers; and in one local paper four different editions—Kelly's being the first—were advertised in the same column.[26] Two sermons preached on the occasion were published following Sunday services on August 17 and 24, respectively.[27]

In the end, it was Kelly's edition which won the test for accuracy and popularity. A hundred years later his edition was reprinted in a series of famous trials.[28] From a recent book which reexamines "the red barn mystery," this incidental intelligence is here offered as a postscript.

According to the legal practice of the day, Corder's body was "dissected and anatomised"; a copy of Kelly's book was bound in a piece of Corder's skin specially tanned for the purpose. It is still on view at Moyse's Hall Museum in Bury St. Edmunds, together with the murder weapons. Corder's skeleton was given to the West Suffolk Hospital where it is still used today for anatomy lessons.[29]

25. Published by John Fairburn, Broadway, Ludgate.

26. The other editions were: one published by George Foster, 68 Leadenhall Street, London; Knight and Lacey's; and one by T. D. Dutton of Bury St. Edmunds.

27. *The Privileges of the Righteous, and the Woes of the Wicked* (Ipswich: S. Piper, 1828) and *The Condemnation of Sinners Opposed to the Divine Pleasure; or, God's Expostulations with the Wicked* (London: Holdsworth & Ball, 1828), respectively.

28. *The Mysterious Murder of Maria Marten at Polstead, in Suffolk* (London: Geoffrey Bles, 1928). It was reviewed in *TLS* on 19 April 1928.

29. Donald McCormick, *The Red Barn Mystery: Some New Evidence on an Old Murder* (London: John Long, 1967), p. 18-19.

Reading for the Masses: Aspects of the Syndication of Fiction in Great Britian

Michael Turner

Michael Turner is Head of Special Collections, Department of Printed Books, Bodleian Library, Oxford.

One of the persistent themes of nineteenth-century publishing was the attempt of the more 'respectable' authors to reach the ever increasing public of the lower classes. . . . In spite of the enormous circulations achieved by some of the better authors through part publication during the eighteen-forties, it was only in the fifties that they began to realise that there was still [as Wilkie Collins pointed out], an 'unknown public' in the buyers of penny periodical literature, which promised 'a great, an unparalleled prospect' for 'the coming generation of English novelists.'[1]

The economic advantages of a larger audience naturally appealed to authors. This was the period when the respectability and professionalism of authorship were being firmly established. It is true that the best authors were able to make hitherto unheard of amounts of money, but the great majority of writers had to work hard for their livelihood; and, with an ever-increasing awareness of the nature of the property which they were creating for themselves, they were continually on the lookout for new ways of marketing this property and thus increasing their returns.

By the 1860s it was clear that the real secret of reaching the masses lay in cheapness, as, for instance, Edward Lloyd and G. W. M. Reynolds had

1. For a general account of the various Tillotson enterprises see F. Singleton, *Tillotsons, 1850-1950, centenary of a family business.* (Lancashire: Bolton & Co., 1950).

shown with their penny periodicals and part publications. Consequently, it was through the increasing number of penny and halfpenny provincial newspapers that the better authors at last began to reach the limits of the nineteenth-century fiction market.[2]

In October, 1880, a "Quarterly Reviewer" wrote:

> Reference has already been made to the practice of sundry weekly newspapers of publishing novels by popular authors in short installments. This custom is steadily increasing, and has now become a very important feature in provincial journalism. Occasionally, though not very frequently, it happens that the author is able to make arrangements with the proprietors of three or four journals to take his story in "flimsy," and set it up in instalments as he transmits it. This, if he can manage it, is unquestionably the most profitable plan for the author. He gets probably half a guinea a column from each of the four journals to which he will send his work for simultaneous publication; and as each instalment will consist of about two columns and a half, he practically sells the first edition of a three-volume novel—twenty-six instalments—for £136 10s.; less expenses, say £130 net. The book still remains his property, and it is not merely new to the great mass of circulating library readers, but is more valuable than a MS., inasmuch as its printing can be done at a much lower cost. As a general rule, however, these arrangements are made by one of the firms which deal in stereo-matter, such as the National Press Agency . . . and Messrs. Cassell, Petter, and Galpin. . . .
>
> Outside London there are two or three firms which supply stereo-matter, the principal being that of Messrs. Tillotson and Sons, of Bolton, in Lancashire, the originators of this system in the provinces. These gentlemen have the credit of being amongst the most enterprising of their craft in England. . . . Their great business, is the supply of stereo-matter, which they manufacture on a large scale, and supply at very low prices. Of this matter no small part consists of serial novels, the demand for which is so great that they can afford to retain the services of authors of reputation, and to pay them high prices for their work.[3]

Before taking a closer look into the workings of the Tillotson fiction syndicate, here is a very abbreviated account of its rise and fall.

In 1850, John Tillotson (1821-1906), the eldest son of the Rev. Samuel Tillotson, a Primitive Methodist minister, became the owner of

---

2. M. L. Turner, "Tillotson's Fiction Bureau; agreements with authors," in *Studies in the Book Trade: in honour of Graham Pollard* (Oxford, Bibliographical Society, 1975), pp. 351-78. On pp. 352-53 is an account of the surviving records of the Bureau, which will explain subsequent references.

3. *Quarterly Review* 150:533 (1880).

a printing concern in Mealhouse Lane, Bolton. (Bolton is one of the larger industrial towns of Lancashire, just to the north and west of greater Manchester.) This firm had been founded by Robert Marsden Holden, with the help of his father, in 1827. John Tillotson was apprenticed to Holden in 1834 and, having married his master's sister, he was taken into partnership, ultimately succeeding to ownership upon Holden's retirement.

The announcement of this change in ownership, which appeared in the *Bolton Chronicle* for July 6, 1850, shows the firm to have been well established, with a variety of interests common to the first half of the century. Letterpress printing, stationery, bookbinding, machine ruling, bookselling—day and Sunday school books and prizes being a specialty —are all listed. The business was also a depository for the British and Foreign Bible Society, and a depot for the Religious Tract Society's and Sunday School Union's publications.

It is to John Tillotson's son, William Frederic Tillotson (1844-89), however, that the firm owes its tradition of interest in new ventures, and the introduction of new techniques. Having served his apprenticeship, and having been tested in the management of the new Mawdsley Street printing works, he was given a partnership in 1866. On the 19th of March 1867, he began a halfpenny daily evening paper, the *Bolton Evening News*.[4] Within a few years he was reversing the normal procedure of newspaper development by adding to this a weekly paper. The *Bolton Weekly Journal* was first issued on November 4, 1871.

From this first weekly paper there developed a group of newspapers, which became known as the Lancashire Journals Series.[5] The series consisted of a number of newspapers devoted to specific localities around Bolton, each with its own manager and reporting staff, but printed in Bolton and under the general control of the editor of Tillotson's newspapers.

4. W. F. Tillotson later discovered that his idea for a halfpenny daily newspaper had been anticipated by what Mr. Singleton describes as a "shipping gazette, published at South Shields." I take this to be the *North and South Shields Gazette and Daily Telegraph,* which first appeared at a halfpenny in Jan. 1864. Although the paper describes itself [*Newspaper Press Directory,* 1864, p. 71] as taking "great interest in promoting of everything bearing on the prosperity of our Commercial Marine, . . . it gives a 'Shipping Gazette'," it still contained the usual features expected of a local daily newspaper. Tillotson's paper was unique in that it was originally independent of a daily morning or weekly paper.

5. For the "Lancashire Journals Series," see Singleton, *Tillotsons,* ch. 3, and the *Minutes of Evidence taken before the Royal Commission on the Press* for

From its very first number the *Bolton Weekly Journal* carried a serial story, the anonymous "Jessie Melville; or, the double sacrifice" being the first. This was followed by three further anonymous stories running through 1872 and 1873, but on Saturday, June 14, 1873, the paper carried the following blurb:

> In August Next, the Bolton Weekly Journal and District News Will commence the publication, in Weekly Chapters, of An Original Story by that Greatest Living Novelist Miss Braddon, Authoress of "Aurora Floyd," "Eleanor's Victory," "Henry Dunbar," "Lady Audley's Secret," "Dead Sea Fruit," "Run to Earth," "Birds of Prey," Rupert Godwin," "Captain of the Vulture," "Circe," "Doctor's Wife," "Trial of the Serpent," "John Marchmont's Legacy," "Charlotte's Inheritance," "Sir Jaspar's Tenant," "Lady Lisle," "Lady's Mile," "Only a Clod"—The New Story, upon which Miss Braddon is at present engaged, will be powerfully domestic in interest, full of character, incidents, and movements, and certain to rival the most of her former achievements.—The Proprietor and Publisher of the Weekly Journal and District News has great pleasure in making this announcement. The Arrangement, which he has been so fortunate to make, is necessarily accompanied with very great cost, but is an earnest of the determination to make the Journal in every sense acceptable to its readers.

The checklist of Miss Braddon's work apart, the readers of the *Journal* were clearly in for something special by way of a serial story.

There was little "puffing" in the mention of the "very great cost," for Miss Braddon had been paid £450 for the serial rights alone of her new story, "Taken at the Flood," which after a great deal more publicity began to appear on August 30, 1873. It was more than coincidence that this was also the date of the launching of two new Tillotson newspapers. Indeed, it may have been the case that the purchase of Miss Braddon's story was in the first instance seen as a means of attracting the public's attention to these new journals, for they were both starting up in areas where newspapers already existed.

Nevertheless, if Tillotson was determined to provide literature of this type for his readers, he had to find some way of spreading the heavy costs even beyond his own expanding number of newspapers. Syndication of news and advertisements had become a regular practice in the

Apr. 15, 1948 (Command Paper 7462, questions 9793-9821). There have been many changes in the titles of the various newspapers in this series, reflecting the changing significance of the various districts concerned.

newspaper world, and applying these techniques to the fiction that he bought, Tillotson found a ready market in the rapidly expanding provincial newspaper press of his time.

The pages of the *Bolton Weekly Journal* during the 1870s show that no matter what the original intention behind buying "Taken at the Flood," the move must have paid for itself, for further stories by Miss Braddon continued to appear, and other serials accompanied these by equally popular authors: Florence Marryat, B. L. Farjeon, Capt. Mayne Reid, Dora Russell, Joseph Hatton, Jessie Fothergill, Mrs. Linnaeus Banks, George Manville Fenn, and Wilkie Collins, along with others by lesser-known writers. Between the purchase of "Taken at the Flood" in the middle of 1873, and the end of 1879, William Frederic Tillotson spent at least £5,465 on stories appearing in the *Bolton Weekly Journal* alone.[6] The enterprise was certainly not starved of capital in its early years, and it may be that the Bureau was subsidized by the jobbing printing side of the business.

As mentioned earlier, the *Quarterly Review,* by 1880, considered Tillotson to be the dominant provincial factor in this area. A few years later another commentator on the British newspaper scene confirmed this view:

> Within recent years a special feature of the Provincial Weekly Newspaper has been the "Story." And to Messrs. Tillotson, . . . is due the credit, to a great extent, of introducing this feature into the columns of the Weekly Press. The plan generally adopted is this: Negotiations are commenced with an author for the purpose of producing a novel, and if an arrangement is come to Messrs. Tillotson purchase the exclusive right of the author's work; they then offer to supply the same to newspaper publishers (on the payment of a stipulated sum), in weekly instalments. The novel is often supplied in stereotype ready for printing, or printed slips are sent to the newspapers purchasing, for their own printers to reproduce.[7]

The 1880s saw an expansion in the business, with a growing number of impressive names being added to the "List." It was possibly during this decade that the Bureau offered its best collection of authors. To those already mentioned as providing material during the seventies were added

6. This figure does not include all the stories in the *Bolton Weekly Journal* during these years, and there may have been other stories with which Tillotson dealt but which did not appear in the *Journal.*

7. *About Newspaper: chiefly English and Scottish* (Edinburgh: St. Giles Printing Co,. 1888), p. 40.

Rhoda Broughton, Charles Reade, "Ouida," Justin McCarthy, William Black, Mrs. Oliphant, Thomas Hardy, Walter Besant, Bret Harte, Rider Haggard, Baring Gould, and Hall Caine.

About 1888 Tillotson visited the United States, in order to study newspaper developments, and took the opportunity of establishing a New York office for the Bureau; in the eighties he had also employed an agent in Berlin and translators and foreign compositors in Bolton, in order to supply the stories in the form of *feuilletons* to the continental press.[8] Meanwhile the Bureau had become one of the main suppliers of feature material throughout the British Empire. At this point, at the height of his success, William Frederic Tillotson died, after a short illness, on February 19, 1889.

In the twenty-two years since the founding of the *Bolton Evening News,* Tillotson had made his mark on the newspaper world. Not only had he established an important group of newspapers and an international literary agency, he had also helped to revolutionize the author's approach to marketing his output. This task had not always been easy, as an article in the *Writer,* promoted by Tillotson's death, pointed out:

> At one time a famous author would have rather scorned the idea of letting his stories run out in driblets in provincial newspapers, with the daily or weekly tag, "To be continued." That he knows now is in great part due to the efforts of William Tillotson, and the establishment which he has founded in his Lancashire town under the high-sounding but perfectly legitimate title of "Fiction Bureau." . . . When the story-writer came to see that he might have at once from a newspaper circulation as big a sum, and sometimes a bigger sum, than he would be paid by a publisher, and that without parting with any of his rights over his story when it appeared in book form, he opened his eyes and began to consider. Ultimately he was pretty sure to take the money, and presently would have not little satisfaction in seeing his work coming out regularly in a multitude of papers.[9]

On his death William Frederic left a widow, Mary, sister of William Lever, afterwards the first Lord Leverhulme, and three sons, John, James, and Fred. W. F.'s father, John, had retired from the business although he lived until 1906. John, the son, had only entered the firm during the previous year, while James and Fred were still at school. The burden of the business, therefore, fell upon Mary Tillotson (1844-1918) and

8. *Pubisher's Circular,* v. 52, no. 1235 (1 Mar. 1889), p. 224.
9. "The Fiction Bureau," in *The Writer, a monthly journal for literary workers,* v. 1, no. 6 (Apr. 1889).

William Brimelow (1837-1915). Mary Tillotson evidently shared many of the qualities which went into the making of her brother Lord Leverhulme, and her determination during the years following her husband's death must have been largely responsible for the continued success of the business. William Brimelow was a journalist by profession and had joined Tillotson in 1871 as the editor of the *Bolton Evening News.* By all accounts he was another remarkable person who had played no small part in the earlier years of expansion.

The ingredients of the Fiction Bureau were all present at the time of William Frederic's death, and the 1890s were a period of consolidation. The list continued to grow and Henty, Hornung, Bennett, and Wells appeared for the first time; but it was during these years that a number of lesser lights were recruited, who were to prove the mainstay of the Bureau for many years to come: J. Monk Foster, Arthur W. Marchmont, Robert Buchanan, Maggie Swan, Annie S. Swan, John Strange Winter (pseud.), William Le Queux, Richard Marsh, Fergus Hume, and John Oakley.

James Lever Tillotson (1875-1940) joined the business in 1892, and from 1893 was responsible for the Bureau. It was at this time that Arnold Bennett, the editor of *Woman,* began to write for Tillotsons; he gives a not altogether flattering picture of Lever Tillotson, who was in the habit of calling on him in order to sell him stories for the magazine:

> I was struck, as I have been before, by the man's perfect ignorance of what constitutes literature, and by the accord which exists between his own literary tastes and those of the baser portion of the general public. . . . I asked about Eden Phillpotts. The reply was: 'He has recently put up his price and we think it is too high. Besides, the sound of his name is against his success with us—Phill-potts.' A curious criticism [comments Bennett]. But in another year, if I mistake not, Tillotsons will be glad to pay him more than his present price—the comparatively small figure of five guineas a thousand words.[10]

Perhaps Lever Tillotson had more humor than Bennett gave him credit for, and one cannot resist the comment that it was precisely the accord between Tillotsons and the "baser portion of the general public" that made their business so successful. Bennett, of course, was right about Phillpotts and the day did come when he had to be paid ten pounds per thousand words.[11] Whatever Bennett's strictures on Lever Tillotson there

---

10. R. Pound, *Arnold Bennett, a biography* (London, Heineman, 1952), p. 114.
11. "The Matchmaker." 4,000 words. £40 for world serial rights on Jan. 15,

is no doubt that he was hardworking and efficient in his job, and Bennett soon came to appreciate the money he himself could earn through the Bureau.

In 1899, John Tillotson joined the board of Lever Bros., and a greater burden fell onto the shoulders of Lever Tillotson in Bolton. He advertised for an editor for the Bureau, and the job was given to a young man called Philip Gibbs, later to become Sir Philip Gibbs. Gibbs did not stay in Bolton for too long. In November 1902 he left to begin his meteoric career in Fleet Street, though both he and his wife were to market much of their writing through the Bureau for many years.[12]

After Gibbs's departure the department was largely run by Fred and Lever Tillotson as well as by Robert Sheppard (1870-1934) and Isaac Edwards (1876-1941), both of whom had joined the firm as boys and were to rise to directorships.

Although it cannot be said that the Bureau declined between 1900–14, there is a feeling that perhaps the greatest days had passed. Increasingly, Tillotsons had to deal not with authors themselves, but with their agents, men like A. P. Watt, J. B. Pinker, and Curtis Brown. There was not really the necessity for two middlemen. Also the monthly journals were proving more attractive to the better authors and, although the Bureau continued to introduce writers of merit to the world, the bulk of their programs were made up of second- and third-rate writers.

The First World War undoubtedly provided a real challenge to an enterprise such as the Fiction Bureau. The *Programme* for 1916 stated the problem, and then neatly turned it into a selling point:

> The past year has proved a trying and a searching time for the newspaper world. Faced with a two fold problem—the necessity of providing space for war news and allied topics, and the expediency of reducing the size of issues because of paper difficulties, editors have been compelled to sacrifice features which had an established place. The choice has not been easy. Some editors discarded fiction temporarily on the ground that war news was stranger and more exciting than fiction could be; but the majority of those who took this view soon discovered their mistake,— the mistake being nothing more nor less than a wrong conception of why fiction is so widely read in the family newspaper.

1908. Published July 4, 1908. [Tillotson Archives, Notebook 'D', p. 38; & Ledger 'A', p. 2]. This was slightly exceptional. Five guineas was his usual price for British and Colonial rights.

12. Sir Philip Gibbs, *The Pageant of the Years, an autobiography* (London, Heineman, 1946), p. 31.

Fiction appeals because it holds the mirror up to life; quickens the imagination; delights the heart and stirs the pulses; and refreshes jaded nerves. No war news could accomplish these things, and so newspaper readers (especially women throughout the land) soon felt the need of fiction, not less, but more. They asked for it, clamoured for it, as a distraction from the exhaustion and depression produced by reading of the tramp of armies, the loss of life, the destruction of homes. Men and women are reading fiction to-day more eagerly than ever before to keep themselves cheerful, to retain a healthy outlook, to feel that life still holds some measure of joy and hope.[13]

However, the number of provincial newspapers had begun to decline before the war and many more did not recover from the paper restrictions which were enforced in 1917. The potential market was shrinking. In 1921 the *Programme* faced up to another problem: "It is held by some that the cinema has displaced the novel," but again an optimistic twist is given, and the customers are assured that the demand for fiction is really growing.

Literature, itself, was going through a revolution. In the earlier years the best authors had told good stories, and this was what the masses enjoyed. The twenties however, were the years of "The Waste Land" and *Ulysses*. The London *Times* wrote:

A clever Irishman has written a sort of novel which contains no story whatever: and some profess an opinion that novels from which plot has been diligently eliminated are destined to be the novels of the future. It may be so. But in that case the philosophers will have to come to the help of a world deserted by its proper entertainers and supply the missing stories. For stories the World will, somehow get.[14]

Needless to say, Tillotsons' publicity left the world in little doubt as to where it could get its stories.

The year 1927 produced yet another competitor to the weekly install-ment, the wireless.

In spite of all these distractions from newspaper reading, Tillotsons continued to stress the popularity of fiction, and fiction in serialized form. But this popularity in its turn caused problems, and possibly the major one, for the stiffer the competition for serials the higher the price. In 1925, they themselves had reported a case where "so keen was the com-petition for the latest novel of a widely-read author that £12,000—a

13. *Programme* 1916.
14. Quoted in *Programme* 1923.

record price—was paid for part serial rights."[15] The total cost to Tillotsons of the twelve serials offered in the same programme had been £1,363 —the most expensive having only cost £250. The Bureau had obviously fallen a long way out of the top league.

For another ten years Tillotsons carried on, but the death of Robert Sheppard in 1934 must have marked the passing of an era. Tillotsons' only chance to remain in this field would probably have been to move the Bureau to the capital and concentrate on becoming a major literary agency, but they were not willing to abandon their provincial newspaper base. So, as they had always been good businessmen above all else, on March 14, 1935 the following letter was sent out:

> Dear Sir, We desire to inform you that from the 31st March, 1935, we have disposed of our entire newspaper syndicating business to Newspaper Features Ltd., 23, Fleet street, London, . . . and have transferred to them all copyrights we possess in serials, short stories, articles, &c., including all matter in our 1935 programmes. . . .

We should now take a closer look into the workings of the syndicate. Because of the nature of the surviving records much of the evidence which will be quoted is from the early years of this century, but there is no reason to suspect that this does not reflect a true picture of the practice of Tillotsons over the last quarter of the nineteenth century. Moreover, I have already published a report on the nature of the agreements which Tillotsons made with their authors, and it is through these agreements that one learns the most about the acquisition side of their business.[16] Before looking at the methods of distribution, I will quickly review my principal findings.

First, let us turn to an article published by *Lippincott*'s, written just after William Frederic's death:

> There is some doubt as to which of our English papers was the pioneer of the new departure; but the late Mr. Tillotson, . . . was undoubtedly the first to grasp its significance and conceive the idea of supplying country and colonial papers with first-class fiction at prices which they could afford to pay. In theory, the system which he adopted was simplicity itself. He bought the serial rights of a story from some well-known author, and then arranged with sundry newspapers for its simultaneous publication in their respective districts. He was thus a wholesale dealer,

15. *Programme* 1925.
16. See Turner, "Tillotson's Fiction Bureau," for a fuller account and documentation of the material summarized in the following paragraphs.

and his profit consisted in the difference between the price which he paid his authors and the sums which he received from his subscribers. In practice, however, the business was attended with difficulties which could only have been successfully surmounted by a man of Mr. Tillotson's exceptional energy and executive skill. Before he could sell his story he had to buy it; and as at the outset he dealt solely with authors of repute, he had often to wait a twelve month for the first instalment of "copy," and even then he was not always sure of getting it.[17]

The agreements certainly show that the vast majority of transactions were with individual authors, and that the authors usually signed their own names to those agreements. Those who wrote under pseudonyms normally used their own name on the contract, but sometimes indicated the name under which the story should appear. As I stated earlier, the emergence of the literary agent was one of the factors against which Tillotson had to struggle. Again, there was no necessity for two middlemen; there are consequently few agreements made through agents, though occasionally they do appear, or an author in making his own agreement would give an agent's name as an address.

Tillotson bought some of his material "second-hand" from other newspaper proprietors, publishers, and syndicates and, when he had finished with such rights in a story that he wished to use, and yet still controlled further rights which he did not wish to use, he would dispose of them to other publishers. On one occasion the film rights in a novel by Lady Troubridge were sold to the Agenzia Letteraria Internazionale in Milan for £75, when exactly the same rights had been bought from the author only twelve days previously for £63. On another occasion, Tillotsons acted as agent, on a 10 percent commission, for the sale of one serial use of Mary Cholmondeley's "The Prisoners" in the *Morning Leader* and its associate paper the *Northern Echo* of Darlington, on behalf of Hutchinsons & Co. who owned the rights. But as far as can be judged from the available evidence, these two cases appear to be exceptions.

Authors were often warned against making contracts with other parties and "their administrators, executors, and assigns, or successors, as the case may be." This form is very rare in the Tillotson agreements; yet the continuity of the agreements does not seem to have been affected by either the death of William Frederic, in whose name the earlier agreements were made out, or by the sale of the business to Newspaper Features in 1935. Indeed the letter announcing the sale had specifically

17. W. Westall, "Newspaper fiction," in *Lippincott's Monthly Magazine* 40:77 (1890).

stated "we . . . have transferred to them all copyrights we possess in serials, short stories, articles, &c."

Payment was invariably a sum of money and quoted as such, though clearly worked out on the basis of a rate per thousand words. Occasionally, besides the monetary consideration, Tillotsons would return various rights in other stories, which they had previously acquired, but for which they no longer had any use.

Normally, payment was made by cash or bill on one, two, three, or even four dates, which were either specifically stated, or bore some relation to the signing of the agreement; the delivery of the manuscript; the publication of the first installment; the publication of another, named, installment; or the publication of the last installment. A great deal of variety exists in the nature of this part of the agreement. As the business was predominantly concerned with serial rights rather than volume rights, royalty agreements were rare, and must be regarded as unusual for Tillotsons.

The nature of the rights which Tillotsons acquired were also diverse. The earlier years saw the greatest variety; after the turn of the century the formula was generally for serial and translation rights; and, after the First World War, it was invariably for no more than British and Colonial serial rights (excepting the North American continent). One of the printed proformae used for the earlier agreements stipulated that the author was selling "the Copy and Copyrights of a Manuscript," which undoubtedly meant what are now described as absolute rights. On some agreements this was unamended but, as time went on, more and more of the agreements were altered and limited in one or another of the following ways:

> Serial, Serial right outside America, Serial, American & Continental, Serial & translation rights, Serial Publication . . . such story not to be published by me in volume form for six months after Serial publication has first taken place, Newspaper, even Newspaper publication in both Hemispheres, [remaining rights], except bookrights, excepting the right of subsequent volume publication in this country, except the right of Dramatisation, and the privilege . . . of publishing this story in any collected edition of his works.

These limitations also occur in combinations. Very often the right to exclude subsequent book rights is associated with the sale of serial rights in one form or another.

The author did not always make an outright sale of his rights; sometimes he merely leased them, or allowed Tillotson to use them for a limited period of time, or even for a particular occasion.

Well known are the problems of English authors in the United States before the Copyright Act of 1891, and the practice of supplying advance sheets as a means of overcoming some of those difficulties. The early agreements show that William Tillotson made quite a business out of this practice; as noted earlier, he had established a New York office on his visit to the States shortly before his death in 1889. Before 1891 most of the fuller agreements are based on this formula. The proforma spoke of the right to "supply Advance Sheets to the United States of America," but it was actually headed "Publisher confined to serial issue except in the United States." That American volume rights were included in this right to supply advance sheets appears to be confirmed by the fact that on purchasing "The Mahdi" from Hall Caine, the deal included the return of the American volume rights of "The Prophet," for which agreement had been made for the lease of the serial rights "together with the right of supply to America of Advance Sheets." I have never followed up the American side of the business, but of course, if it did not come to an end with Tillotson's death in 1889, it did two years later with the new Copyright Act.

The general practice after the First World War was to exclude all North American rights. Canada presented a special problem. Though a signatory of the Berne Convention, Canada was in some respects at odds with it, and with the 1911 British Act which applied throughout the Dominions. Because of the virtual control of the Canadian market by American publishers, provision had been made to allow the supply of literature which otherwise might not have been available. Thus the Canadian Act of 1921, for example, granted the right to license the printing of a book and the publishing of a serial in Canada to persons other than the owners of the copyright. In practice this meant that British authors reserved the Canadian rights and made special arrangements for them, usually by means of American publication followed by Canadian registration.

Very occasionally, Tillotson bought English language continental rights. But long before Tillotson entered the market, English language rights for the continent of Europe had been practically a monopoly of the Firma Tauchnitz of Leipzig, whose "Collection of British Authors" was familiar to continental travelers from 1841 up to the beginning of the Second World War. Where rights for the publication in the English language were concerned, therefore, some formula along the lines of

"Tauchnitz edition excepted" was fairly common in the Tillotson agreements.

The agreement would usually state the length of the novel, and further define it in terms of a number of installments of so many words in average length. The publisher usually asked for some guarantee of originality, together with a safeguard against any possible legal proceedings. The method of delivery was usually laid down, and it is quite clear that in many cases the serialization may have begun before the complete copy was delivered. The author was often called upon to correct proofs and this was seen as a duty or a right depending on the author's attitude. When the story remained to be written, the general locale and period might be stipulated. A synopsis of the story might have already been approved, or one might be called for. In later years it was commonplace for the agreement to contain such a sentence as "The said company shall also be at liberty to make such alterations in the story as the exigencies of serial publication in their judgment require." A similar freedom was often allowed in the matter of the title. Acceptance of such clauses clearly depended on the bargaining power of the author.

Tillotsons sometimes made an attempt to write into the agreement some commitment on the part of the author to offer subsequent work to them, and in later years several authors were clearly on a type of regular contract, guaranteeing to supply stories at regular intervals over a number of years. On the other hand, authors often asked for guarantees regarding the dates of first serialization, in order to facilitate the arrangements relating to subsequent volume publication and the distribution of other rights.

Now let us turn to the distribution side of the Bureau's business, again beginning with the obituary of W. F. Tillotson:

> The caterer of fiction for newspapers of course arranges with his customers that they shall have the exclusive right of publication in their own district. This would seem seriously to restrict his field, and to prevent him obtaining a return on the large sums which are now paid to the great novelists for whose works a demand has been created by their supply. But the caterer may have plenty of time of recoup himself. He will first let out the story to papers willing to pay a large sum for first publication. Then, when the rights of these papers are exhausted, he will sell the right of publication to a humbler set of newspapers at a lower price, and so on till the poorest papers in remote regions are reached, and even they need not be without their share of the best fiction of the day, although they must wait longer for it. The caterer quotes his price per story of so

many newspaper columns. He prints it from the author's manuscript, or publishes advance sheets and sends it out in proof-sheets to his customers, taking care that no one gets a time preference over the other. To some newspapers the story is even sent out in stereotype blocks ready for the local printing press.[18]

Having acquired his material, Tillotson had to arrange the serials and stories into a "Programme," which fixed the date of first publication for each item. About September of each year Tillotsons sent out a *Programme,* in which the serial stories to be offered during the course of the following year were listed according to the date of publication of the first installment. Anything from eight to fifteen or sixteen serials might be offered: the average length being about thirteen installments, allowing for a rough grouping to permit a choice of between two to four stories each quarter. The choice was greater in the years preceding the First World War than in those following, though it increased again towards the end of the 1920s. The programmes sometimes contained a short biographical note on the author, and always a brief synopsis of the serial, or its opening chapters. A more or less complete run of these programmes from 1905–32 has been seen, and so the arrangement of serials during that period is certain. For the earlier years, the *Bolton Weekly Journal* provides a sort of guide, though such an approach gives no indication of the choice available; nor does it necessarily produce the date of first publication, for, at least as far as some matter was concerned, Tillotsons' own papers were twelve months behind the programme in 1910.

No central records survive concerning the sale of any of the serial stories. Such evidence does exist for some of the short stories, the so-called storyettes, and other feature material. There is no reason to believe that the procedure in the case of this material was in any way different from that generally adopted for the sale of the serials.

A selection of names of those authors who were to be included in the series of short stories and storyettes was given in the *Programme,* but the details were not printed in full. Two parallel series of short stories (4,000-5,000 words) and storyettes (2,000-3,000 words) were arranged. In each there was a story for every Saturday throughout the year. Sometimes they were offered in two six-month series; sometimes in four three-month ones.

A broadside, containing the text and illustration to Frankfort Moore's

18. *See* n. 9 above.

"Her Advocate," may give a clue as to how these series were publicized. This story was the first, or lead story for a series of short stories first published in 1904. Beside the text of the story, the broadside gives a complete list of all the other stories in that series, and it is possible that all lead stories were available in this form, acting as bait for the series.

Each Christmas the firm offered a supplementary supply of seasonal stories and feature material, and special programmes were sent out for these. In addition other material was available throughout the year. In 1909 there was at least one article for each Saturday of the year beside the regular fiction series. In 1901 Tillotsons claimed that about 30 new serial stories and over 300 short stories of various lengths were published by them each year.[19] In 1909, there were 15 serials and 174 other stories or articles. Also, an always increasing amount of material from previous years was available.

Tillotsons almost certainly furnished newspaper offices in every town of the British Isles with their programmes, and apparently with considerable success. There was hardly a part of the country that was not covered, at some time or other, with Tillotson material. It must be remembered that the sale of the story was based on the exclusive right to publish it in a given area. Thus the heavily populated counties, with the largest number of distinct individual urban areas, offered the greatest scope; while one sale might be sufficient to cover a sparsely populated agricultural county, served by one widely distributed newspaper.

The arguments for publishing fiction in newspapers were straightforward. They were "(1) To raise the rank of a paper; (2) To increase the circulation." Increased circulation made the newspaper a more attractive proposition to the advertisers. Documented figures concerning the effects of fiction on the circulation of newspapers are impossible to find, but stories are not:

> A case is familiar to journalists, where the stories of one man are said to have raised the circulation of a country newspaper from 30,000 to nearly 150,000. An evening newspaper proprietor states that when he began to publish stories daily, his advertisers as well as some other people took serious objection to his course. It was not considered "the respectable thing" for a daily evening paper to do. Now that they have seen the effect on the circulation they have come around to the proprietor's opinion.[20]

19. *The Progress of Newspapers in the Nineteenth Century* London, Tillotsons [1901].

20. *See* n. 9 above.

Short stories gave a newspaper variety and additional interest, but the serial had an extra advantage. This was put to promotional use in the difficult years after the First World War:

> From the editor's point of view the special value of the serial story is that it is the one link between successive issues. It gives the reader something definite to look forward to in next week's issue, and that is the surest way of securing continuity of interest and purchase. Thus the paper which runs a serial has a great advantage over those which do not.[21]

Tillotsons' annual claims for the never-failing interest in a good story were well founded and, until the newer media of the wireless and the cinema made popular entertainment more easily available, the penny and halfpenny newspapers were the surest way for fiction of this type to reach the largest audience. Added to this natural appeal was a highly competitive situation in the provincial newspaper world, with most towns having at least two rival papers. Thus, once serialized fiction had become acceptable to newspaper editors and readers, no paper which wished to remain competitive could afford to be without it.

The matter was available in printed form as copy; in stereo demy-columns of thirteen, fourteen, and fifteen [pica] ems in width; or in matrixes or molds of the same dimensions. Contemporary accounts seem to agree that it was Tillotsons' provision of stereotype columns that was responsible for their far-reaching success in attracting the more remote smaller papers and journals. Unfortunately, the documentation does not survive to ascertain the extent to which these columns were bought in the early years. After 1908, it appears to be only a small minority that continued to buy the matter in this form, though Tillotsons continued to supply it throughout their entire history.

A small plant for casting such columns was by no means a heavy item of capital expenditure.[22] As early as 1870, such a plant could be bought for as little as seven or eight pounds, and the purchase of stereotype must not be taken to mean that the purchaser was not himself equipped to perform the necessary tasks. It can only be assumed that some saw no point in resetting and casting matter which was already available in a

21. *Programme* 1921.

22. *Newspaper Press Directory* (1870), p. 192. T. Tather of Hull: "News-column stereotyping machines £7.7s. Everything complete. . . . Moulds can be sent through [the] post to a branch or any other concern, which would be a considerable saving in wages, when two establishments are kept; or local news can be exchanged with other proprietors at a distance. No furnace or casting room required, as the whole can be worked in a few feet of space, and so simple that a boy can cast with a few hours practice. To sum up, it saves wages, time, and type."

form which could be incorporated into existing makeup. Molds were more commonly bought during the period from 1908, but if the absence of any notation regarding stereos or matrixes in the ledgers means that printed copy was the form in question, then that was by far the most common.

The question of the charges made by Tillotsons for their material is the most difficult to face. It would appear that each instance was a matter for individual negotiation, based on the author(s) concerned; the circulation figures and area covered by the purchasing newspaper; the form in which the matter was to be supplied; the dates on which the material was to be published; and, presumably, whether or not there was any competition for the use of the material within the same area. The absence of dependable circulation figures, together with these factors and the wide variation in the amounts paid for seemingly the same material have made it impossible to discover any standard figure which formed the basis for negotiation, though there must have been some rule of thumb. It would appear that in the shorter fiction series the authors involved were not a factor in determining the price, though this could not have been the case in the sale of serials. So far as it is possible to follow the same newspapers buying the complete series for publication at the earliest dates over a number of years, it is clear that once a price had been agreed upon, it remained the regular price for the newspaper concerned, unless there was a general increase.[23] The cost (payments made to the author) to Tillotsons of the first series of short stories for 1909 was £189 11s.; sales before the end of 1908 amounted to £180, a further £18 from Sydney on January 5, 1909, ensuring that this series had more than paid for itself [in this limited sense] three days after the first publication date.[24] Tillotsons had earned at least £318 for this series by the time they sold the business in 1935; and Newspaper Feature earned another 15s. from the *Illustrated Police News* for the use of Austin Philips's "The Murder at Silchester Post Office" in January 1937.[25] The records show that most of the series had either covered the payments to the authors or were on the point of doing so by the publication date of the lead story.

Any attempt to produce detailed figures of the purchase costs of the serial stories for those years in which we have knowledge of the *Programme* is somewhat unsatisfactory because of the difficulties of equating agreements which have no titles, or titles which never appear to have

23. Between 1908-28 such increases took place in 1918, 1920, and 1921. See Ledger "A."
24. Notebook 'D', pp. 44-45.
25. Ledger 'A', f.3.

been published, with the stories that appear in the programmes. Also there are too many gaps in the information to arrive at anything more than a general impression. I mentioned earlier that the twelve serials offered in 1925 cost £1,363. Twelve out of the sixteen offered in 1905 cost £1,074 15s. As the total costs of the short stories showed relatively little change over the years, it might be assumed that Tillotson maintained a similar attempt at stability over the years in other fields. In this case, the average cost of the serial series during the second half of the firm's history would have been between £1200–1400 a year.

I attempted to trace all the actual appearances of the two series of short stories which first appeared in 1909, and this showed that the stories remained on the market long after the year in which they were originally published.[26] The last appearance noted for either of these series was that just quoted in the *Illustrated Police News* on January 7, 1937. Both series sold regularly into the early 1920s, and the second one ran at length in the *Cotton Factory Times* during 1934–35. The ledger clearly shows that at the time of the transfer of the rights to Newspaper Features in 1935, the stories in these and all the other series were carefully checked to see if they were still suitable for sale, and if the molds were still serviceable. Many of the stories from the 1914–18 period, for instance, were rejected because of the relation of their subject matter to the war.

It can be shown that Tillotsons acquired, either explicitly or through the purchase of "entire" copyrights, a large number of volume rights. The use to which these rights were put is something of a mystery. In some cases they were returned as part payment for later purchase, but this was not very common; and yet Tillotsons themselves do not appear to have gone in for volume publication on any scale. The volume forms of the novels which can be found appear over the imprints of the more usual publishers of fiction, especially those specializing in the cheaper issues. The main problem is that not nearly enough of the serials have been located in volume form. The reasons for this may be varied. In the first place there was clearly a section of the material published in the newspapers that proved unsuitable for publication in volume form. Secondly, when the novels did achieve such publication, they probably appeared only in the very cheap paperback series, which rarely got cataloged individually by libraries which were large enough to have them in the first place. A great deal of work needs to be done on the listing of

26. See Appendix III, section B, in my thesis "The Syndication of Fiction in Provincial Newspapers, 1870-1939," Oxford, 1968. Copy deposited in the Bodleian Library.

such series, before much that is useful can be said about them. Finally, I suspect that there were often changes in title, and perhaps in the author's name, between newspaper serialization and volume publication. This was undoubtedly more likely the cheaper the volume intended, and the nearer the market for that volume was to the market supplied by the newspaper serialization.

An agreement with "Ouida" for *A House Party* specifically stated that "the Publisher agrees to publish in handsome Library form not later than October 1886."[27] The earliest edition, dated 1887, was published by Hurst & Blackett, but the Bodleian copy is date stamped on December 1, 1886, which shows that the volume was available in time for the Christmas trade. The printing of the Hurst & Blackett edition was done by Tillotsons. It seems that when a particular publisher prints a first volume edition, they usually were the original syndicators of the novel.

One attempt was made to provide a more regular outlet for these rights. On September 2, 1886, " L. T. Meade" made an agreement with Tillotson concerning a novel entitled *Beforehand:* "The said Publisher may print and publish the said story in his series known as 'Tillotson's Shilling Fiction,' and Publish the same in the said series on or before the Thirtieth of June Next."[28] The *English Catalogue* duly reported the publication of the volume in June 1887, in Tillotson's Shilling Fiction series, but the imprint was that of George Routledge. *Beforehand* was the seventh, and perhaps the last, in a series which had begun in 1885 with the publication of a novel by "Ouida," *A Rainy June*. However, the latter and the second of the series were published by John and Robert Maxwell; Routledge apparently taking over the series with the third volume.[29] All the volumes were printed by Tillotson in Bolton. They had a uniform wrapper on the shilling issue, but were also available in cloth at one shilling sixpence. The arrangements under which the Maxwells and then Routledge published these volumes have not been discovered, but John Maxwell was the husband of Mary Braddon, and it is probably through Tillotson's close business association with this lady during the seventies and eighties that the contact was made. The Fiction Bureau, with its regular supply of fiction would seem to have been the ideal basis for such a series, but it appears to have come to nothing. The publication of only seven volumes in two years does not indicate that William Frederic was putting much effort into the series at this stage, but it is possible that it

27. Bodleian Library, Ms.Eng.misc.f.395/1, f.28.

28. Bodleian Library, Ms.Eng.misc.f.395/1, f.74.

29. I was originally assisted by Miss Margaret Selley of Routledge & Keegan Paul Ltd., for help on this point. So far only seven titles have been traced.

was a casualty of his death in February 1889. On the other hand, it may be that the series never really flourished in what was after all a fiercely competitive market.

Tillotson's Fiction Bureau played an important role in several fields. First, it developed the techniques and widened the scope of syndication. Until the 1870s syndication had been used mainly for news and advertising. William Frederic Tillotson was largely responsible for applying the system to fiction and feature articles. In its turn, syndication was to some extent a factor in the growth of the provincial press during the second half of the nineteenth century, and one of the chief ways in which this growth was sustained.

Second, the large scale marketing in serial rights which resulted from such an enterprise helped to establish the trend towards the division of literary property into different types of publishing rights. This division involved the author in more and more business matters, until it became inevitable that a third party would emerge whose function was to be the manager of this entrepreneurial side of literary activity. Although the literary agent has often been cursed by the author, there is no doubt that his presence has ensured the development of the professional author, freeing him from tedious business routine while at the same time obtaining the maximum returns possible for the work done.

Finally, because the authors also benefited in a general sense from the tremendously increased exposure obtained through the Fiction Bureau, they were at last able to reach the limits of the literate classes.

The masses of the lower working classes were introduced to fiction of a somewhat higher order than that to which they had been accustomed. Although this fiction may have left a lot to be desired from the literary point of view, there can be no doubt that it did at least establish the habit of reading in many thousands, and possibly some hundreds went on to more worthwhile things. Even if the chief function was escapism, this was no mean service in the harsh world in which most of the readers found themselves.

If Tillotson's activities appear to be an obscure byway of Victorian publishing history from our viewpoint, we must remember that it was the judgment of William Frederic's contemporaries on his death that he "did more to popularize fiction with the masses than could have been achieved by a century of ordinary effort."[30]

30. Westall, "Newspaper Fiction," p. 77.

J. Ross Robertson— Publisher: Aspects of the Book Trade in Nineteenth- Century Toronto

Douglas Lochhead

Douglas Lochhead is Davidson Professor of Canadian Studies, Mount Allison University.

Subjects such as printing and publishing and popular reading tastes in nineteenth-century Canada are just beginning to receive scholarly bibliographical attention. A heightened awareness of the country's history and its culture has prompted such investigations. The results, even after a number of somewhat tentative beginnings, have revealed some distinctively Canadian as well as international trends. One printer and publisher who dominated the Toronto book trade in the last decades of the nineteenth century and who set trends in book publishing and marketing new to Canada was John Ross Robertson.[1] His imprint variously appeared as J. Ross Robertson, 55 King Street West (and then later, 67 Yonge Street), Publisher.

This study, the second account of a large work-in-progress, endeavors to examine book trade practices in Canada as developed by Robertson.[2] It will be seen that they are similar in some ways to those of nineteenth-

1. This paper is based upon a larger work-in-progress which is devoted to J. Ross Robertson's book publishing activities and which is being carried out by Marion Press of Toronto and myself. Valuable assistance has also been received from Elizabeth Hulse of the University of Toronto's Thomas Fisher Rare Book Library.

2. For a first account, *see* "John Ross Robertson, Uncommon Publisher for the Common Reader," in *Journal of Canadian Studies,* vol. 11, no. 2, May 1976, p. 19–26.

century Great Britain and the United States. It is also possible to observe, with a touch of speculation, that Canada, through the efforts of Robertson, was beginning to develop something like a popular culture through Robertson's daily newspaper, the *Telegram,* and the hundreds of cheap paperback books which brought fiction and romance to Canada's readers at rock-bottom prices.

It will be helpful to examine some of the evidence about Robertson, the man, as well as Robertson, the publisher and promoter. Robertson's feud with Mark Twain over copyright, for example, led to some international tensions, and out of it all there came about a surprisingly large reading public with a taste for the popular fiction of the time. That much of it was pirated from living American authors meant nothing to the buyer of the latest title from one of the many Robertson cheap editions.

Who is this who has been described as "a superb journalist, an intimidating benefactor, a dedicated but haphazard collector of Canadiana, a man who loved children but distrusted adults," and was considered by more than a few as a "cantankerous old bastard?"[3]

Although as a benefactor Robertson's name is prominent, this intriguing man, born in 1841 and who died in 1918, is not well known. It is reported that at the graveside of John Ross Robertson the mourners experienced some sense of regret, but the feeling was not unanimous. Evidently Robertson was many-sided, a man of many guises, a man at whose death the people who had thought they had known him found that only part of him was within their experience and understanding. As his biographer asks, "who really knew John Ross Robertson, when all was said and done?"[4] His progress as publisher and promoter of books will be highlighted here.

The evidence of the Robertson "aspect" in nineteenth-century Canada lies for the most part in the files of the newspaper Robertson founded, the *Evening Telegram.* Because he was "endlessly busy," he was negligent in the compilation of his personal and business papers. As was mentioned, he collected Canadiana but, unfortunately, not his own publications. Indeed, relatively few of his books, largely paperback, have survived, and one must clutch at every shaky piece of bibliographical evidence there is: advertisements in newspapers (invariably the *Telegram*) and lists of titles on the wrappers of those of his books one is fortunate enough to locate. There are also occasional references in bibliographical and literary records, but these last are disappointingly few.

3. Ron Poulton, *The Paper Tyrant: John Ross Robertson of The Toronto Telegram* (New York: Clark, Irwin, 1971), p. 4.
4. Ibid., p. 3.

From the lack of hard bibliographical evidence it is perhaps reasonable to expect that what will emerge from this work on Robertson will be, as intimated earlier, a social or cultural history of publishing in nineteenth-century Toronto, perhaps concentrating on popular reading taste, all with strong bibliographical overtones. The bibliographical evidence will be absorbed in the social commentary but it is realistic to state, at this point, that much of this evidence will be statistical in form and chronological in arrangement. For instance such parts of the larger study would include: (a) a chronological study of the titles, which would include notes about other editions which Robertson pirated; notes on the authors, noms de plume; the promotion of the books and their library locations; (b) indexes of authors, titles, and an attempt to arrange the titles within the many series of books advertised by Robertson.

Prominent in any study of nineteenth-century book publishing should be, where evidence is available, the whole matter of promotion and advertising of titles. The importance of publishers' records cannot be overemphasized, but it is a rare event when such documents are found. What we do have as evidence, cautious as we must be of it, are the advertisements. In Robertson's case the message is the advertisement, and one must lean on the very considerable and prominent space he devoted to book promotion during his active book publishing years from 1877–90. Examples of his advertisements help to outline the Robertson book industry. His desire to launch a successful paperback business is there for all to read. It would be interesting at some point to measure the advertising lineage which Robertson gave over to his campaigns to promote his titles.

On Friday, February 23, 1877, the *Evening Telegram* carried a large display advertisement on the top right-hand corner of its front page announcing Robertson's first venture into paperback publishing. Under the heading "New Publication" the prominent notice went on to describe the book that was "forthcoming" the next day:

Complete and Unmutilated Edition./
Moody's Anecdotes./ Every One Should
Have A Copy./ Popular Edition./ Price:
Ten Cents./ For Sale By All Newsdealers
in the Dominion./ Wholesale Agents/ Toronto
News Company, Jordan Street./ Robertson's
Ten Cent Edition/ Contains exactly the same
amount of reading contained in the Fifty and
Seventy-Five Cent American or Canadian
Editions/ Be Sure and Ask for Robertson's
Cheap Edition.

The last line, in fact the whole advertisement, might well, with some slight alterations, have been used for promoting cough syrup. At least it has that certain ring about it.

Turning attention to the *Evening Telegram*'s advertising copywriters in this initial prepublication advertisement, one sees immediately the kind of promotion they thought best to apply. There is, for instance, the statement, "Complete and Unmutilated Edition." Here, Robertson was, by inference, saying that some other editions of *Moody's Anecdotes* that might be on the bookstands were likely to suffer from abridgment. The wide scope of distribution indicated is an important point, suggesting the popularity of the *Anecdotes* "By All Newsdealers in the Dominion." Then, in this and later advertisements, there was a comparison of prices with American and Canadian editions: "Price . . . Ten Cents" and "Contains exactly the same amount of reading contained in the Fifty and Seventy-Five Cent American and Canadian Editions." In this initial advertisement, so typical of Robertson's brand of merchandising, three names of editions are mentioned: "Popular Edition," "Robertson's Ten Cent Edition," and "Robertson's Cheap Edition." This indiscriminate labeling of editions does little to help the bibliographer in his attempt to arrange systematically the many Robertson titles in their proper series. Over the next thirteen years Robertson went on to establish ten-cent, fifteen-cent, twenty-cent, twenty-five-cent, thirty-cent, forty-cent and fifty-cent editions as well.

To follow *Moody's Anecdotes* through its promotional stages in the *Evening Telegram* helps one to trace the pattern of Robertson's endeavors to sell his paperback wares. In this same issue of the *Telegram,* in a one-column advertisement, the following text for a day-of-publication notice appears:

> New Publication/ Complete and Unmutilated
> Edition/ OUT TODAY./ MOODY'S/ ANECDOTES./
> CHEAP POPULAR EDITION,/ TEN CENTS./ This
> edition contains same matter as original
> American Edition./ Ask for Robertson's
> Edition./ For Sale by all Newsdealers./
> Trade supplied by Toronto News Company,/
> Jordan Street/.

Just to add to a growing confusion, two more possible new editions or series are mentioned in this short advertisement—"Cheap Popular Edition" and "Robertson's Edition."

The following day there appeared another large display advertisement of the same size as that which appeared the day before, but with a revised and more sensational message. This notice stressed the line "PRICE TEN CENTS" in forty-eight-point type. In thirty-point type, as opposed to the six-point type of the previous day, Robertson made the claim that his edition "Contains exactly the same amount of reading contained in the Fifty and Seventy-five Cent American or Canadian Editions." This same large advertisement appeared on page one of the *Evening Telegram* on Monday, February 26, and Tuesday, February 27.

As was Robertson's custom with many of his paperback titles, it was published in serial form in the *Evening Telegram* concurrently with the sale of the book. At the heading of the first installment which appeared on Wednesday, February 28, just five days after the book was announced as both "forthcoming" and "published," there was the following text: "These Anecdotes and Illustrations may be had complete in book form from any news dealer in the Dominion. Price ten cents. Ask for Robertson's edition." One must doubt this statement for a number of reasons, including the rapidity of distribution it suggests was possible among all the confederated provinces.

Moody's Anecdotes, written by Dwight Lyman Moody (1837–99), appeared in fifteen serial installments between the dates Wednesday, February 28, 1877, and Thursday, March 29, 1877. This book was derived from Moody's revivalist preaching. Why it was selected by the strong-minded Toronto Presbyterian as the first title to be published is not known. The titles which followed it were most certainly not in the revivalist tradition but perhaps Robertson did feel it set a certain tone for his future publications. More likely the reason for its appearance under such auspices was its availability: it was free for the taking.

It is interesting to note that the majority of the writers whose works were to appear under the Robertson imprint were women novelists whose works were best-sellers in the United States. From about 1850 on, women writers appear to have largely dominated the fiction successes in New York, Boston, and other publishing centers. Robertson's titles would not have appeared out of place in any of these cities. It was a time of the hard sell. Best-sellers were made in the 1850s and 1860s, as Susan Geary has pointed out in a penetrating analysis of the publishing industry of that time.[5] In her article, "The Domestic Novel as a Commercial Commodity: Making a Best Seller in the 1850s," Geary begins her paper with a quotation from the *American Publishers' Circular*:

5. Susan Geary, "The Domestic Novel as a Commercial Commodity: Making a Best Seller in the 1850's," Papers of the Bibliographical Society of America, New York, vol. 70, no. 3, 1976, p. 365-93.

> . . . if the truth be told in relation to the large sale of certain publications, their publishers owe more of this success to startling advertisements, liberal discounts, and newspaper puffery, than they do to the intrinsic value of the books themselves.

Startling advertisements and newspaper puffery were part of Robertson's approach to successful book marketing. The ridiculously low prices when compared to American editions also account for his success.

Bringing marketing techniques from the 1850s and 1860s into the late 1870s in Toronto, Robertson also must have been aware of the outburst of cheap book publication which had begun about 1870 in the United States and which lasted until the early 1890s at least. His known book publishing period coincides with this time almost exactly and soon became part of that explosion. What brought his book publishing to an end and caused the decline of other cheap libraries was, of course, the International Copyright Act of 1891.

While J. Ross Robertson was beginning his publishing business in Toronto, such firms as T. B. Peterson; George Munro; Norman L. Munro; Richard Worthington; Hurst & Company; Donnelley, Lloyd & Company; John W. Lovell; Belford, Clarke & Company; John B. Alden; and J. S. Ogilvey were turning out such "Libraries" as the *Lakeside Library, Seaside Library, Franklin Square Library, Lovell's Library,* and the *Riverside Paper Series* among others.[6] Of the firms mentioned several were founded by Canadians or had Canadian connections. George and Norman Munro were Nova Scotians, John W. Lovell was from Montreal, Belford and Clarke had Toronto connections. In the 1890s some of these firms collapsed, but some of the best-known names in publishing circles also devoted a part of their activities to the paperback revolution of the 1870s to 1890s: Harper & Brothers; D. Appleton; Henry Holt; Dodd, Mead; and Funk & Wagnalls.

The second title of Robertson's paperback publishing ventures was a novel by Bret Harte entitled *Thankful Blossom.* This new book was first announced on February 28, 1877, in prominent front-page advertisements, just five days after *Moody's Anecdotes.* Bert Harte's *Thankful Blossom* was priced at three cents. Incidentally, during this same period the price of a single copy of the *Evening Telegram* was two cents.

Robertson showed his hand early by trying to create an instant bestseller. Just one day after the book was announced, readers of the *Tele-*

6. For an interesting account of these companies, *see* Raymond Howard Shrove's *Cheap Book Production in the United States, 1870 to 1891* (Urbana: Univ. of Illinois Library, 1937).

TWENTY CENT BOOKS

MY OPINIONS AND BETSY BOBBETTS

By Josiah Allen's Wife—Designed as a beacon light
to guide women in life, liberty and the pursuit of
happiness, but which may be read by members of the
sterner sex without injury to themselves or the book.
22nd thousand. No book ever published in Canada has
had such an extraordinary sale as "Betsy Bobbetts"
[it is simply misleading advertising copy in 6
point-type albeit. The sales figure must apply to
the American market and just what 'extraordinary sale'
means can be anyone's guess]

THE STILLWATER TRAGEDY

By THOS. BAILY ALDRICH

QUEENIE HETHERTON

By Mrs. Holmes. Her new book—186 pages—complete.

A STRANGE DISAPPEARANCE

By ANNA KATHERINE GREEN

"Wilkie Collins would not need to be ashamed
of the construction of this story . . ." *Evening Post*

A TIGHT SQUEEZE;

Or, the Adventures of a Gentleman,
Who, on a wager of ten thousand dollars, undertook
to go from New York to New Orleans in three weeks,
without money, as a professional tramp.

EQUAL TO ANY OF MARK TWAIN'S

Full of Life and Adventure. Startling Scenes of Real Life.

TWENTY-FIVE CENT BOOKS

HER WORLD AGAINST A LIE

By FLORENCE MARRYAT

LOVE WORKS WONDERS,

By B.M. CLAY

A WOMAN'S TEMPTATION

By BERTHA M. CLAY

PEERLESS CATHLEEN

By CORA AGNEW

CURSE OF EVERLEIGH,

By ELLEN CORWIN PIERCE

THE WIDOW BEBDOT PAPERS

Reprinted for the first time—from the original edition

ROBERTSON'S THIRTY CENT NOVELS

HOW TO GET STRONG AND HOW TO STAY SO
  By WILLIAM BLAIKIE

BARRIERS BURNED AWAY
  By E.P. ROE

A BETTER ATONEMENT
  An ideal romance   By BERTHA M. CLAY

THE ROOT OF ALL EVIL
  By FLORENCE MARRYAT

MILDRED
  By MARY J. HOLMES

BEULAH
  By AUG. J. EVANS

A MAD MARRIAGE
  By MAY AGNES FLEMING

SILENT AND TRUE
  By MAY AGNES FLEMING
  12th 1000

A TERRIBLE SECRET
  By MAY AGNES FLEMING

THE HEIR OF CHARLTON
  By MAY AGNES FLEMING

FAITHFUL MARGARET
  By ANNIE ASHMORE

LADY LEONORA
  By ANNIE CONKLIN

THE ACME OF CHEAPNESS

MARK TWAIN'S GREAT BOOK
THE INNOCENTS ABROAD!
214 Pages for Thirty Cents
  The Best Value for the Money ever given to the Public!
MARK TWAIN'S MASTERPIECE
A TRAMP ABROAD

The above list sufficiently indicates that Robertson was not dealing with authors or editorial problems, but simply the publication and merchandising of a wide selection of authors nearly all of whom were American. It was unabashed borrowing on a large scale.

Robertson and his copywriters were not above bombarding the faithful reader's eye as this front-page advertisement will show. It appeared in the *Evening Telegram* of March 4, 1881:

Ready To-day.
ONLY TEN CENTS
ONLY TEN CENTS
ONLY TEN CENTS

"My Wayward Pardner."
"My Wayward Pardner."
"My Wayward Pardner."

BY JOSIAH ALLEN'S WIFE
BY JOSIAH ALLEN'S WIFE
BY JOSIAH ALLEN'S WIFE

SPLENDID STORY   100 PAGES   TEN CENTS

Robertson's books representing "The Acme of Cheapness" continued to be advertised almost daily throughout the 1880s.

In our work underway an effort is being made to account for the serial appearances of every novel which appeared during Robertson's approximately fifteen years in the book publishing business. The majority of the books he published appeared in daily installments in the *Evening Telegram*. As mentioned earlier, in some cases the novel would appear first in installments to be followed after a few days by the announcement that the entire book was published. Perhaps this was one of Robertson's ways of whetting the appetite of his daily readers. There is no pattern to the insertion of his installments however. Some would begin to appear the day the full novel was published; other series would appear, sometimes at long intervals after the book had been published. In any case, in whatever form, it was free copy which Robertson could use to fill the columns of the *Evening Telegram*, which in the 1880s enjoyed a readership of over thirteen thousand and which exceeded the combined circulation of his rivals the *Globe* and the *Mail*.

As mentioned at the beginning of this paper, the lack of evidence in book form makes for serious bibliographical difficulties. It is reasonable, though, to make use of information from the advertising columns of the *Evening Telegram* in order to retrieve some indication of an almost lost literature. Purists would have it that this sort of retrieval is largely speculative. To some extent this may be true, but when titles published by Robertson in the late 1870s were still being advertised ten years later it seems reasonable to conclude that his high-pitched advertising copy proves that he published extensively during a very prolific publishing period in Canada's history. And actual titles in book form do make their appearance from time to time.

The immediate work before us now is to prepare a full list of his titles and authors and to chart the rate of publication between 1877–90.

It is hazardous to estimate the number of titles published by Robertson. On the basis of counts made during some of the years between 1877-90, which average about twenty-five titles, a complete set of his various series would amount to approximately three hundred and fifty titles; not an insignificant body of literature and surely one which must be recorded in more detail and analyzed within the bounds of historical bibliography and beyond.

That there were signs that the Robertson book publishing empire was in decline is reflected in this brief but telling notice which appeared in the Toronto book-trade journal, *Books and Notions,* in January 1889, p. 101:

> Robertson's Library; which has been jobbed off in quantities to the retail trade, is now offered to the novel reading classes in some stores at half prices, in others at the tempting rate of 'three for a quarter'.

John Ross Robertson published actively in Toronto over a period of almost thirty years. Conservative estimates indicate that he issued between three and four hundred titles during that time. Through the columns of his extremely successful daily newspaper, the *Telegram,* Robertson promoted his books widely and well. He obviously was aware of the popular writers of the day in the United States and he pirated their works with no obvious twinges of remorse. This ardent Presbyterian businessman was an astute publisher, a promoter of those books he felt would sell.

The *Telegram* had the largest circulation of all Toronto's newspapers. It set the style and created a taste for popular reading among its customers. There is a strong case to be made for Robertson's contribution to what might be described as Toronto's popular culture of the last decades of the nineteenth century.

The Case of the Vanished Victorians

Franklin Gilliam

Franklin Gilliam is the proprietor of the Brick Row Bookshop in San Francisco.

INTRODUCTION

by Larry McMurtry

Ladies and gentlemen; it is to me a matter of rich chagrin that, today of all days, I have to be represented here by just these few pages.

Like most book persons, I am convinced that years of earnest study have given me a full, just, and respectful appreciation of the rare, and I think surely few would contest the claim that Mr. Franklin Gilliam's appearances at the lectern achieve the category of high—if not absolute —rarity.

Indeed, from what I can discover, *The Bay Psalm Book* comes to the auction block about as readily as Franklin to the lecture hall. Neither phenomenon is apt to occur more than once or twice in a lifetime, and, once speech or sale is consummated, there is no guarantee—nor indeed even the likelihood—that the like will ever be seen or heard again.

You who are fortunate enough to be in Toronto had thus best listen and learn, while you have the chance.

As for me, I find it just possible to console myself with the thought that I may have already been told as much as I am meant to comprehend of what Franklin knows about the gathering of nineteenth-century books. Many years ago, when the Brick Row Bookshop was to be found on a pleasant street in Austin, Texas, I often spent hours in its cool and usually silent aisles, staring at the nineteenth-century books that had just been gathered.

Larry McMurtry, the well-known American novelist and proprietor of the *Booked Up* book store in Washington, D.C., was unable to be present at the conference to introduce Franklin Gilliam. He thus sent the manuscript of his introduction to Toronto and it was read for him. Because of its witty and cogent evocation of an antiquarian book business it seemed appropriate to include it here.

In those days the Brick Row managed to suggest the very *beau ideal* of bookselling as a way of life—particularly if one's ideal inclined at least a bit toward the Edwardian. If one happened to arrive at the premises in the morning hours one could count on finding an atmosphere that was, at the very least, relaxed. Indeed, somnolent would be the more accurate word. This state of dormancy would usually be broken around noon, when Franklin might emerge from his chambers in pajamas and robe and cast a skeptical eye at whatever newspapers had found their way in during the night.

At about that same time, his confrere and cataloguer Anthony Newnham would appear from somewhere and the day's work would begin. Anthony, in life-style at least, seemed to represent the earlier and rowdier half of the shop's favorite century. His life at times seemed to be an imaginative extension of Lord Byron's, whereas Franklin, in his capacity as head of the firm, strove to merge the best qualities of Lord Acton, Samuel Butler, and Jerome K. Jerome.

Once the two were fully aroused from the stupor of morning, bookish activity commenced and continued at a measured pace throughout the afternoon and evening. There were interruptions, of course, for an appropriate amount of ingesting and imbibing, and, from time to time, when the bright sun and tedious chatter of Austin became too much, even longer interruptions known as buying trips.

I could never quite comprehend the necessity for these buying trips, for the shelves of the shop were already jammed with items so recondite that there was no reason to suppose they would ever sell. But buying trips there were, and these, like the daily operations of the shop, were conducted with a good deal of measure and equipoise. All movement was of course by train, and the bookshops visited seemed to have been chosen mostly for their proximity to acceptable rail lines, restaurants, and hostelries—and in such regard standards were by no means low. Weeks might well pass in this stately fashion, and then Franklin and Anthony would suddenly reappear in Austin, not visibly fatigued from their travels, and set about opening the scores of parcels that would by this time have accumulated, mute but intriguing evidence of their progress through the bookshops of many states, and several nations.

The contents of these parcels were, to my naive eye, an education— if only into the refinements of specialist bookselling. I was at the time a fledgling novelist, naturally much absorbed by the literature of my own century. It was thus little short of shocking to find D. H. Lawrence jostled off the shelves by Mrs. Martineau, to have Hemingway and Joyce crowded out by Praed, Pater, and Patmore, and to find Faulkner having to compete for space with Edward Eggleston and Joseph Rodman Drake. In particular, it was a source of sustained wonder to me that so many books could be found that had evidently been published between 1885 and 1915, a period during which, so far as I knew, not much had been written except the more unreadable books of Henry James. That a bookshop would actually care to stock such writers as Meredith Nicholson and Edward Hutton, Francis Gribble, Jucas Malet, Leonard Merrick, and

Mrs. Sedgwick, was, at the very least, something that required thinking about. Was this a noble infirmity, made financially viable only by the desperation and gullibility of a few librarians who, because they happened to be stuck in Nevada, Saskatchewan, or the maritime provinces, couldn't really hope to get anything else; or was it, rather, a case of two enlightened booksellers gallantly banking on their own predilections and thus seeing to it that at least a few universities were saved from the shallow prejudices of the age?

That is a question to which I have given generous, if periodic, allotments of thought ever since, finding happily, that it is one of those questions about which one feels no pressing need to reach a conclusion. Even more happily, I can now invite you to turn your attention to the man who prompted it in the first place: the proprietor of the Brick Row Bookshop, Mr. Franklin Gilliam.

My first inclination toward this discussion was to dwell upon certain nineteenth-century authors who seemed to me to be neglected by collectors—private or institutional—whether relatively or entirely. There are certainly enough of these authors, as the series (now in the neighborhood of fifty) of bibliographies published from time to time in the *Book Collector* demonstrates. It should be noted, however, that the majority of them are neither novelists nor Victorians, and so, given my personal predilection for Victorian fiction, I began to brood more and more upon a fact really obvious upon reflection: namely, the demonstrable rarity of first editions in this field, in almost any condition. So, rather than discoursing on uncollected or, more accurately, uncollectable nineteenth-century authors, I have chosen to discuss "The Case of the Vanished Victorians."

Throughout his wonderful career as a collector and bibliographer in the fields of Gothic and subsequently (among other things) of Victorian fiction, Michael Sadleir stressed a dominant fact of life. In the pioneering *Excursions in Victorian Bibliography,* he warned that "copies of three-volume novels by writers of reputation are hard to find at all, and very hard to find in anything of condition. Nevertheless, when found they are often cheap. And then, when one is bought, there comes the reading of it."[1] Still true, excepting, alas, the middle factor. (One wonders, however, how many prizes could still be acquired for the $16,000 recently achieved by William Carlos Williams's first book?) Twenty years later, in a paper on "The Development During the last Fifty Years of Bibliographical

1. Michael Sadleir, *Excursions in Victorian Bibliography* (London, Chaundy & Cox, 1922).

Study of Books of the XIXth Century," published in *The Bibliographical Society, 1892–1942: Studies in Retrospect,* Sadleir renewed his warning, in a slightly different context:

> The only road to even a partial knowledge of binding variants and secondaries, of cheaper editions in cloth, wrappers or pictorial boards, is the road of experience; and though to travel that road is, for eccentrics of the right sort, a journey of enchantment, it is also a slow and often discouraging one. The early editions of obscure titles, or of books which in their day had virtually no circulation, may be assumed to be uncommon; but the baffling scarcity in 'unimproved' original state of the majority of once popular and well known books of the period of from (say) 1830 to 1880 has to be endured to be believed.[2]

Finally, in 1951, summing up the section of relative scarcities, concluding the first volume of the great catalog of his collection, this supreme collector and bibliographical theorist says:

> In conclusion, I must paraphrase a statement . . . [from his *Trollope, a Bibliography,* London: Constable, 1928], as it is essential that its content be impressed upon the reader's mind and never forgotten. The word "rarity" and its implied counterpart, must be understood in a purely relative sense. With perhaps a half a dozen exceptions . . . no Victorian two- or three-decker in original condition is "common" in the accepted meaning of the word. How should it be otherwise, when we consider that lapse of time, the destructive voracity of the Circulating Libraries, the taste for uniform calf-binding which beset our ancestors and (perhaps as damaging as any) the wholesale pulping of then unwanted old novels which, owing to paper shortage, took place in 1917 and 1918? This same threat again beset us not long ago and in a more acute form; but one must hope that first editions of significant nineteenth-century fiction were sufficiently valued by their possessors to have been withheld from the salvage drives of the years 1939-1945."[3]

Closer to home and nearer in time, Dr. Gordon Ray, in a 1964 article in the *Book Collector,* wrote of his own splendid private library that "the first and largest of my special collections, [that] of minor fiction . . . of all the sections of my library . . . would today be the hardest to dupli-

2. Michael Sadleir, "The Development During the Last Fifty Years of Bibliographical Study of Books of the XIXth Century," in *The Bibliographical Society, 1892-1942: Studies in Retrospect* (London, The Society, 1945), p. 155.

3. Michael Sadleir, *XIX Century Fiction: A Bibliographical Record* (London, Constable; Berkeley and Los Angeles, University of California Press, 1951), vol. 1, p. 373.

cate";[4] he spoke with double authority, for in addition to his personal collecting achievements, he had, in the years following the Second World War, brought together a fine collection of Victorian fiction for the University of Illinois. Combing the United Kingdom from stem to stern for many summers, armed with a *Cambridge Bibliography of English Literature* (CBEL) marked to show the Illinois holdings, he added several thousand volumes a year to their shelves, making Urbana, as a result of very energetic digging, a major center for research in Victorian fiction. To strengthen the printed resources, a substantial portion of the papers of the great publishing firm of Bentley were acquired (some twelve thousand letters and manuscripts), as well as the Grant Richards and H. G. Wells archives.

And finally, writing in the next year for the same quarterly, from a large Victorian house in Cambridge, very full of Victorian novels, Professor Robert Lee Wolff of Harvard tells of his own progress on "the Road to Three-Decker Ruin":

> I have never experienced the kind of windfall that sometimes came Sadleir's way; where he acquired the Bentley fiction file in an afternoon, I have usually had to buy my novels one or two at a time. 'Seen once (and bought) or never seen at all,' the terms in which Sadleir describes his experience with the novels of Mrs. Trollope, can nowadays be applied to the whole range of Victorian fiction. His tables of comparative scarcity . . . today have largely academic interest as reminders of the happy days when he formed his collection . . . Good luck in 1965 consists of finding a decent copy even of *Endymion* or *Felix Holt*.[5]

Not to despair, those who wish to start a career collecting three-deckers can *still* begin with George Eliot's *Felix Holt* (twenty-two copies sold at auction and twenty offered by the dealers listed in the *Bookman's Price Index* for ten years after 1965); or Disraeli's *Endymion* (only seven at auction, one of which was rebound and another a rare proof copy which fetched £140, and a dozen from the booksellers); or, adding a third title to a very exclusive list, *One of Our Conquerors* by George Meredith (nine copies at auction and nineteen in the trade). Beyond this one could reasonably expect to find Meredith's equally ubiquitous *Lord Ormont and His Amynta,* plus a fair number of expensive titles by major hands, but from there on the flow becomes but a trickle.

4. Gordon N. Ray, "Contemporary Collectors XXXVII: A 19th Century Collection" in *Book Collector,* vol. 13, no. 1 (Spring 1964), p. 43.

5. Robert Lee Wolff, "Contemporary Collectors XLII: Nineteenth-Century Fiction I" in *Book Collector,* vol. 14, no. 3 (Autumn 1965), p. 336.

It is clear that there are only a minute number of successful private collectors operating on a broad scale: Sadleir, Wolff, Ray, and Morris Parrish probably constitute the majority. The situation among the institutional collectors is much the same. For them, taking the long view is right and proper, but for the individual, a very high order of determination, stamina, and luck, plus civilized bibliomania to a marked degree are required. Wolff is candid about this:

> Everyone in the 19th century read novels, and the collector comes to feel that everyone wrote them. But unless one selects one must allow the luck of the chase to be one's only guide. The advantage of indiscriminate acquisition is that discrimination can come later, in the reading. In any case, how select? If George Augustus Sala (S[adleir]), why not Edmund Yates (N[ot] I[n] S[adleir]? . . .[And he continues in this vein through several alternatives]. Unable to answer these questions, I have simply declined to follow Sadleir's choice of authors, and have plodded along, collecting them all. Now that I have almost 6,000 novels [this in 1965, and the brilliant plodding continues]—perhaps a little more than one seventh of the entire fictional output of the period, and more than twice as many as Sadleir—all I need is about 36,000 more . . . It has been a long road and a downward one, and I am sure now that it has no end. Searching for the books and finding them is almost reward enough. Cataloguing them after they arrive gives balm and comfort. But the keenest pleasure of all comes when the reading of a novel—preferably obscure or at least forgotten—helps to dispel the heavy mists that separate us from the Victorians, and reveals an artist overcoming the pressures of his society and creating men and women who still live for me in his pages.[6]

This of course is the point of it all, and we are the fortunate recipients now of three books from Professor Wolff based upon his collection (with occasional assistance from an outsider's novel): *The Golden Key* (New Haven: Yale, 1961), a study of George MacDonald; *Strange Stories and Other Explorations in Victorian Fiction* (Boston: Gambit, 1971), investigating occult and neurotic themes in the novels of Bulwer-Lytton, Harriet Martineau, and Laurence Oliphant, together with a most entertaining long chapter on "Some Pleasures of the Chase"; and finally, the recently published *Gains and Losses: Novels of Faith and Doubt in Victorian England* (New York: Garland, 1977). Announced as in the works is a study of the life and fiction of Mary Elizabeth Braddon. Thus continues the tradition of Michael Sadleir, who "never . . . [undertook] the inten-

6. Robert Lee Wolff, "Contemporary Collectors XLII: Nineteenth-Century Fiction II" in *Book Collector,* vol. 14, no. 4 (Winter 1965), p. 511.

sive collection of any author or movement without the intention of ultimately writing the material collected into biography, bibliography or fiction."

Two of these four great private collections have now passed into institutional hands (and it is fair to suspect that the others will one day follow). It is thus instructive to consider their present condition under relatively new administrations. It is twenty-five years since the Sadleir collection arrived at Westwood and the same length of time since the West Coast took its place as one of the few geographic centers where Victorian fiction can be studied in depth. Negotiations were protracted and complex, and the prize was virtually on its way to Urbana, when, at the eleventh hour, a good deal of luck and an act of genuine magnanimity by Dr. Ray sent the collection to the University of California at Los Angeles (UCLA). Much has been written of this coup, and of the subsequent celebrations attending the installation of the collection. The Friends of the UCLA Library marked the dedication ceremonies by publishing the addresses by Frederick B. Adams, Jr. and David A. Randall, together with a foreword by Michael Sadleir, in a pamphlet with cover in yellow-back style, published at "Bruin Court near Sunset Fields," and titled *Revelations of Two Celebrated Book-Snatchers, or, What Victoria Read.* Sadleir wrote:

> I could wish no more suitable home for these books than the shelves of a great American Library, and no more congenial a Library than that at UCLA. Here the books will be *used,* if Adams' advice is taken (as it surely will be), the gaps will be gradually filled and the subsidiary projections of the main collection will be tirelessly followed up. For the vigilance of UCLA need never be relaxed.[7]

Adams also concluded his remarks on a strong note:

> I have no hesitation in pointing out that the UCLA Library has an obligation not simply to preserve this collection, but to keep it alive. It must be constantly nourished, cultivated by scholars, and supported in its natural growth. There are several directions in which it can be expanded, and it is important that the staff of your Library be able to take prompt advantage of unusual opportunities as they arise. But I am not really worried about the enthusiasm and perseverance of Dr. Powell, nor the imagination of the faculty, the Regents, and the administrative officers

7. Michael Sadleir, "Foreword" in *Revelations of Two Celebrated Book-Snatchers, or, What Victoria Read* (Los Angeles, Friends of the UCLA Library, 1953), p. 2.

of this university. After all, they combined to purchase the Sadleir Collection, and a noble deed it was that will not soon be forgotten in the annals of American research libraries.[8]

This confidence was indeed well placed, and—thanks mainly to the patient and generous assistance of Wilbur Smith and Brooke Whiting— I can now proceed to tell you something of the afterlife and development of the Sadleir collection. The current exhibition at the UCLA Research Library illustrates two points vividly: the inspiration and utility provided by the Sadleir collection proper, and the richness of the materials that have been added to it. With its title from Hawthorne, " 'A d——d mob of scribbling women': Nineteenth-Century British Novelists," the exhibit displays first editions, often with accompanying manuscripts, letters, portraits, and significant later editions of 110 female novelists, of whom 37 were not represented in Sadleir's collection, and whose number includes, for example, Anna Eliza Bray, Elizabeth Rundle Charles (author of *Chronicles of the Schönberg-Cotta Family* and several other once extremely popular fictions), Julia Kavanagh, and Mrs. Molesworth (though it must be said that many of the rest do not fall comfortably within Sadleir's chronological boundaries). The prospect for future Sadleir-based exhibits is bright, for there are few aspects of life in the last century that cannot be illuminated from its ranks.

In addition to adding in first edition titles Sadleir lacked, as well as nonfiction by his authors, UCLA has acquired North American, Continental, Colonial, and later English editions, significant variants, ephemera, and, above all, manuscript materials. It is also fair to say that this treatment has been extended to dozens of non-Sadleir authors, and that virtually any nineteenth-century novel is fair game for acquisition. A review of additions, in first edition of novels only, to the ranks of some authors (hard cases all) for whom Sadleir was not overwhelmingly strong would show, for example: Sabine Baring-Gould, for whom the new CBEL lists 43 novels, of which Sadleir had 5, and to which UCLA has added 14; Rolf Boldrewood, the pseudonym of the Australian Thomas Alexander Browne, British Museum Catalogue (BMC) 18, Sadleir 7, UCLA 11; Mortimer Collins (no relation to Wilkie), CBEL 17, Sadleir 9, UCLA 3; Florence Marryat, Captain Frederick's daughter, BMC about 75 (it is not always easy to distinguish adult fiction), Sadleir 12,

---

8. Frederick B. Adams, Jr., "The Sadleir Collection" in *Revelations of Two Celebrated Book-Snatchers, or, What Victoria Read* (Los Angeles, Friends of the UCLA Library, 1953), p. 12.

UCLA 5; G. P. R. James, CBEL approx. 65, Sadleir 13, UCLA 32; Margaret Oliphant, CBEL 95, Sadleir 62 (with the observation in his catalog that "even so incomplete a survey as this would not have been possible without the acquisition of Macmillan's office-file of lesser Victorian fiction; without this exceptional contribution I should have been hard put to it to find a quarter of her output, so utterly do most of her books in original state seem to have vanished"), to these 62 Oliphants, then, UCLA has added a commendable 6; Mrs. J. H. Riddell, CBEL 48, Sadleir 27, UCLA, 1 [and here again an important note to the catalog: "This may not at first sight seem a discreditable series of Mrs. Riddell's books, especially as several of them are in admirable condition. But when it is confessed that the twenty-eight titles here listed (and including both first and later editions) are only a little over half of her output; that eight of the three-deckers came at one swallow with the Bentley collection, and that I have collected her assiduously for more than ten years, the achievement, however meritorious, is revealed as far from exhaustive. Mrs. Riddell is an outstanding example of a prolific and popular Victorian novelist whose books in fine state (and many of them irrespective of condition) seem to have disappeared."]; William Clark Russell, CBEL 67, Sadleir 22, UCLA 25; Thomas Augustus Trollope, CBEL 17, Sadleir 12, UCLA zero.

The success UCLA has had with collecting non-Sadleir authors can be indicated by a few picked at random, though with results that most probably are typical: Julia Kavanagh, CBEL 17, UCLA 17 (a triumph, perhaps as the result of a Sadleirian windfall); James Payn, CBEL 50, UCLA 12; Professor Wolff's candidate Edmund Yates, CBEL 20, UCLA 9. In connection with starting from scratch, it is possible to adduce here evidence from Stanford, where since the late 1950s Victorian fiction in first edition has been diligently garnered. Not seeking every novel published in the last century, they have however pursued the major and minor novelists of CBEL, together with some interesting exceptions, and have now a collection of genuine utility and importance. Here is a sampling of their holdings for a few lesser but significant lights: Baring-Gould, 4 first editions of his 43 novels; Mortimer Collins, none of the 17; Florence Marryat, 1 of the 75; Mrs. Oliphant, 6 of 85; James Payn, 1 of 59; Mrs. Riddell, 2 of 48; William Clark Russell, 2 of 67; T. A. Trollope, 4 of 17; and Edmund Yates, none of his 20. And this with the concerted efforts of a dedicated staff, with a budget adequate to the task, and with many dealers as loyal quoters.

Expansion of the much more selective, but also more exhaustively collected subjects forming the Parrish collection seems to have been considerable, and is described in some detail in two issues of the *Princeton Library Chronicle,* in 1946 and 1956. No doubt reports of further progress will be made in time.

As the twentieth century mercifully begins to fade to its close, one comes to the inescapable conviction that the day is done for a successful entrance into the ranks of broad-scope collection; there will be no more Bentley files, no more Macmillans prepared to allow the collector to fill his gaps from their author-file, and those untouched country houses remotely (or otherwise) situated in the British Isles will hardly swamp the market when and if their remaining hoards of old fiction are disgorged. Waiting for miracles will do little to expand present holdings. The established collections should be—and no doubt will be—steadily augmented as occasion permits; the many three-deckers still in acceptable condition, save for library stigmata, in the stacks of most major institutions must be rescued and cherished (and who knows, sometimes sent where they will do more good); and the existing private collections fondly contemplated. Indeed, as Gordon Ray warned, in a seminal paper on nineteenth-century fiction, read and published at UCLA in 1964 (and to which I am deeply indebted), "It is later than you think!"[9]

Let us look at a more cheerful difficulty, more cheerful because the means of remedying it are within our power, if not always within reach of our purses. First and other significant editions are the working tools of the textual critic and the bibliographer. Indeed, Sadleir, Parrish, Ray, and Wolff have all produced fine books as a result of their own excursions in Victorian fiction, and many more riches remain to be mined. But first one needs a text, any text regardless of edition (in most cases). Access to Westwood, Princeton, or Urbana, to London, Oxford, or Cambridge, the major residences of the handsome originals, is not easy for all, and these same originals must be used with discretion. For most purposes, a reprint will and must do, in those instances where reprints exist. Alas, once the would-be reader descends below the level of the major minor novelists—say Wilkie Collins or Charles Lever or Charles Reade— the prospect darkens. Many of the smaller talents were reprinted—some more than once—in England or America at the time, but these books too appear to have suffered from the same attrition as the first editions, in most cases. Inspection of the fiction shelves of any large second-hand

9. Gordon N. Ray, *Bibliographical Resources for the Study of Nineteenth Century English Fiction* (Los Angeles, School of Library Service, UCLA, 1964), p. 21.

shop in England or America proves this. There also are the once abundant resources of the ever-admirable Tauchnitz Edition ("the only medium by which the text of English novels can get known on the continent," wrote George Eliot). This series was initiated with Bulwer-Lytton's *Pelham* four years after Victoria's accession, and by the end of her last year had published something on the order of 2,500 titles (3,546 volumes to be exact, but they were often multivolumed works), the great majority of them novels by her subjects. These clearly printed and compact little volumes (well-suited to offset reprinting) have also at times textual significance, for as they were authorized, or, later, copyright editions, they at times contained new material by their authors. Simon Nowell-Smith, in the *Book Collector* for Winter, 1966, gives an interesting account of the history of this splendid firm and its relations, usually cordial and profitable, with its writers.

In short then, the commercial supply of reprints is not outstandingly better than that of the first editions, and a look at the holdings of three major university libraries in stack copies, both for reading and as essential protection for their first editions, gives little encouragement. The card catalogs at UCLA, Stanford, and Toronto were examined to see what they could offer for some of the novelists mentioned earlier in another context. For example, for Sabine Baring-Gould, the new CBEL records 43 novels; UCLA has 5 in the stacks, Stanford 2, and Toronto 2; Mortimer Collins, CBEL 17, UCLA 4 (and ironically 3 of these are among the 5 titles not in Special Collections), Stanford and Toronto, both none; Florence Marryat, BMC 74, UCLA none, Stanford 2, Toronto none (and here, for example, Tauchnitz could once have saved the day, for their general catalog of 1913 listed 54 novels); Margaret Oliphant, CBEL 85 (95 says Sadleir), UCLA 13, Stanford 15, Toronto "a number" (their figures were not accumulated by my own efforts); James Payn, CBEL 15, UCLA 4, Stanford none, Toronto 3 (Tauchnitz 47 in the 1913 catalogue); Mrs. J. H. Riddell, CBEL 48, UCLA 9, Stanford 3, Toronto 2; William Clark Russell, CBEL 67, UCLA 27, Stanford 7, Toronto none; T. A. Trollope, CBEL 17, UCLA 2, Stanford 2, Toronto 3; and finally Edmund Yates, CBEL 20, UCLA 1, Stanford 7, Toronto 4 (Tauchnitz, 15). In similar investigations for other novelists of equal mettle, the results were more or less uniform; sometimes, as with Mrs. Braddon or Rhoda Broughton, a fairly good showing was made, but more often than not the figures for available reprints were weak indeed. It seems obvious, given the pitiful supply of reading copies available in the trade, that we must resort to reprinting. Fortunately, some progress is being made: for example, the 120 or so novels that Professor Wolff draws upon in *Gains and Losses* are being reprinted under his editorship by Garland. However, it is generally safe to say that if and when earlier reprints are found, they are likely to be much cheaper than the newer, as is usually the case, but their availability simply cannot be relied upon.

So the sad litany ends, with the observation that it is a particularly painful irony that the most stimulating and fruitful collector of our century should have worked in the one field most certain to doom to frustration any hope of great achievement by private or institutional collectors. Michael Sadleir, considering at the beginning of his collecting career the achievements of the great collectors of the past, while surveying possible new worlds to conquer, saw the futility of following in their footsteps: "the great mutations of the world were over; that to glean where the giants had reaped could no doubt instruct and stimulate—but would still be no more than gleaning." There are still collecting worlds to conquer, as we all know, but not this one. Uncollected? Yes, but not because they deserve it; uncollectable, because they have vanished.

Two American Book Collectors of the Nineteenth Century: William Loring Andrews and Beverly Chew

Robert Nikirk

Robert Nikirk is Librarian of the Grolier Club in New York.

To characterize book collectors in nineteenth-century America, I have chosen two examples with very different temperaments and of differing achievements: William Loring Andrews (1837–1920) and Beverly Chew (1850–1924). This approach is much more interesting than a survey of collecting which can be had by looking into the few books on the period, and the reasons for choosing these two attractive but contrasting collectors will presently emerge.

The library of the Grolier Club is doubtless as good a collection of materials for the study of book collecting in the nineteenth century as exists anywhere. In addition to standard histories, less well-known privately printed books, and booksellers' and auctioneers' catalogs, the Club has an archive dating from its founding in 1884. This remains a virtually unmined resource for studying its activities of all kinds. There is also much material in these files which add to the biographies of early Grolier members, many of whom figured prominently in the artistic and social life of late Victorian New York.

But in the cases of Andrews and Chew, there are specific materials which provide unique insights into their activities as collectors. These priceless materials are the real starting point for this paper because I am convinced they have never been used before.

After the death of Mrs. William Loring Andrews in 1930, the Grolier

99

received as a bequest the scrapbooks and notebooks of her husband. These consist of seven small folios begun, seemingly, around 1880, but incorporating materials saved from years before.

The Andrews scrapbooks and notebooks contain correspondence and all manner of ephemera relating to his privately printed books, bibliographical articles from journals and newspapers, obituaries, invitations, much relating to his long trusteeship at the Metropolitan Museum of Art (including an invitation to the unwrapping of a mummy), conservation in the Adirondacks, feeding Boer children, clubman activities, and many other matters.

As for Beverly Chew, there is also a special hoard of material which led me to choose him. After his death in 1924, his brother sent to the Grolier Club a large collection of letters written to him by his closest bookish friends, beginning in the mid-1880s and continuing up to the time of his retirement to his native Geneva, New York, in 1920. They were placed in a print case and probably never looked at again until I unearthed them (while looking for something else, of course). This archive contains letters from many eminent Grolier and other contemporaries such as Samuel Putnam Avery, John Kendrick Bangs, Theodore Low DeVinne, Robert Hoe, Charles Eliot Norton, Harry Elkins Widener, A. W. Pollard, T. H. Wrenn, and a galaxy of others.

It is difficult for us today to realize that in January 1884, when a group of nine New Yorkers gathered in a Murray Hill parlor to discuss the state of the arts of the book in the United States, that they were about to embark upon something entirely new. Before the Grolier Club was founded, there was no focus for bibliophilic interests in New York. The Metropolitan Museum was fourteen years old and not particularly progressive in outlook. There were no other museums worthy of the name and few art exhibitions of any kind. It is important to keep in mind that for forty years the Grolier held as many art exhibitions as it did rare book and manuscript exhibitions.

The enthusiasm with which the early Grolier members undertook all manner of club activities in the midst of otherwise busy professional lives is clearly demonstrated in the working files for exhibitions and publications which still exist. Their up-to-date and progressive outlook is remarkable for an era which is thought of as staid. The first exhibition of Japanese prints in New York was held at the Grolier, a reflection of the artistic rage of Paris at the moment. French posters were first seen there, with care taken to include American work in the genre. Commercial bookbindings were considered early on—their high quality perhaps the result of Grolier agitation in the field. William Blake emerged for the public as a poet and artist of consequence through Grolier exhibitions and remained a special interest, as a look into a Blake bibliography would prove. Up until the time of the Second World War, *all* the exhibition materials were borrowed from members, though owners were never identified on labels, a commendable policy which persists today.

The publications, all of a high quality, came thick and fast. Some became the standard work on their subjects for years to come, until academic scholarship took over and supplanted the role of the collector and gentlemanly amateur.

Andrews and Chew were avid participants in all this activity from the very beginning. Andrews was a founder and is said to have chosen Grolier's name as the club's own. Both served as president, having prepared for the post by arduous committee work. Andrews even served on a special commission in 1885 to investigate the admission of women as members, an idea not to be realized until May 1976.

William Loring Andrews was born in New York City in 1837, the descendant of a New Haven settler of the 1630s. Andrews's passionate love of his native city determined the most significant path of his collecting life, that of preserving books, drawings, and prints illustrative of its history. In this he was preeminent and his obsession eventually constituted a real contribution to the study of New York's history. One result of his collecting was that he inspired I. N. Phelps Stokes to prepare his great work on the iconography of Manhattan.

Andrews seems not to have attended college but instead entered the family hide and leather business. At age twenty-three he married Jane Elizabeth Crane and eventually had two boys. One died at age fifteen, the other died while a senior at Yale. Andrews himself died, age eighty-three, a symbol of "Knickerbocker" New York, in March 1920.

Beverly Chew was born in Geneva, New York, in 1850, his father having settled there after graduation from Hobart College in 1845. Why Alexander Lafayette Chew, a native of New Orleans, came to Geneva and Hobart does not now seem to be known. At any rate, in 1849 he married a local heiress, Sarah A. Prouty, from a well-established, upstate family. Beverly Chew also retained a lifelong affection for his birthplace, an aristocratic neo-classical town at the head of Seneca Lake. He also attended Hobart, class of 1869, and in later years was a major benefactor of the college. His abiding love for English literature undoubtedly flowered at Hobart, which was, and is, an Episcopalian college. Chew was a devout and active layman all his life.

In 1872 he went to New York to work for Simons and Chew, a brokerage house. He soon moved to the Metropolitan Trust Company and by 1900 was a well-known banking figure. Beverly Chew was not a lifelong bachelor, as some think, but married Clarissa Pierson of Ionia, Michigan, sometime after 1872. How this came about remains a mystery. They had no children and she died in New York in 1889. Chew retired in 1920 to a spacious Italianate house (of which the Grolier Club is lucky enough to have several large photographs) and died in 1924.

Apart from the very important collection of everything concerning the history of New York, Andrews collected thousands of interesting books without a sharp focus in view. In his *Gossip About Book-Collecting* of 1900, he said:

> In a modest way I have run the entire book-collecting gamut. I am so tenderhearted towards anything that bears the semblance of a fine or rare book, that I have yielded to the blandishments of all sorts and kinds.[1]

So his bookcases at 16 East 38th Street, at the corner of Madison Avenue, where he resided all his life, were filled with illuminated manuscripts, incunabula, sixteenth- to eighteenth-century French and English illustrated books, Aldines, Elsevirs, Bodonis, and fine examples of ancient and modern bindings. Andrews seems to have constantly weeded out and added better examples. This we can deduce from his own handwritten library catalog of 1867 with its watercolor title page and illuminated initials done by himself. This catalog, now in the Grolier Club, contains 830 items, nearly all of them written through with a large "Sold" and a price. Few books remained in his library which were there at the outset. The dispersal of all this will be considered later in some detail.

Beverly Chew, on the other hand, was the epitome of the collector with a sharp focus. English literature of the sixteenth and seventeenth centuries was his field and he was a pioneer in appreciating the minor figures of these centuries and forming collections of their works. His knowledge was unsurpassed and widely appreciated.

As I learned more and more of what Andrews and Chew collected, the question of where they bought their books became one of increasing interest. Chew never left the United States and Andrews seems to have traveled abroad infrequently. However, from the correspondence in the Andrews scrapbooks we know he dealt with Ellis & Elvey, James Bain, and especially Bernard Quaritch. He also followed English auctions

---

1. William Loring Andrews, *Gossip About Book Collecting* (New York: Dodd, Mead & Co., 1900), p. 61.

carefully; many of his most interesting books came from the sales of Syston Park, Hamilton Palace, and Michael Wodhull. He probably was not altogether easy to deal with. A long 1889 letter from Ellis & Elvey explains in a pained fashion why he should put his bids in the hands of a well-established bookseller and not with those representing themselves as "American agents" at English sales. They close by proposing how they will spend £150 of his money for a manuscript once at Hamilton Palace.

Having early in his collecting life conceived a typically nineteenth-century preoccupation with Aldines and Elsevirs, and having published a handsome private catalog of his Aldine holdings in 1885, one wonders if Andrews gulped or smiled when he pasted into his scrapbook this undated clipping from the London *Saturday Review:*

> One of the earliest symptoms of bibliomania is a passion for Aldines and Elsevirs. The young patient generally labors under the delusion that all books from the great Venice and Leyden presses are of equal value. Novels encourage this delusion; they always represent learned professors as "rich in Aldines and Elsevirs."

Chew's correspondence shows another possible source which is revealing. Robert Hoe, writing to Chew in January 1900, says: "Quaritch's son writes me that he has sent a lot of books. They number about 50 and amount to nearly 800 pounds in value. There ought to be some good things among them—enough for a small selection. Will let you know when they arrive so you may have a look at them." In other words, Hoe was accustomed to receiving large lots of books from which to make a selection; perhaps Chew shared in this bounty.

Though Andrews had links with the English and French trade (through the agency of Samuel Putnam Avery, the art dealer and bibliophile), and Chew almost certainly with London dealers, most of their books seem to have been bought in New York.

In one of the more readable of Andrews's privately printed books, *The Old Booksellers of New York* (1895), he specified his sources: William Gowans, Joseph Sabin (who is said to have sold over $1 million worth of books between 1864–74), John Bradburn, C. S. Francis, T. H. Morrell, McElrath and Bangs, Calvan Blanchard, Samuel Raynard, Charles B. Norton, and John Doyle. Chew also dealt with these, in addition to a newer generation of booksellers such as Leon & Brother, A. L. Luyster, C. L. Woodward, Francis P. Harper (older brother of Lathrop Colgate Harper), E. F. Bonaventure, William Evarts Benjamin, J. W. Bouton, James Osborn Wright, Dodd, Mead & Co., and others.

Both Andrews and Chew were professionally well located to spend money with the booksellers. Up until the turn of the twentieth century, the booksellers were located on the northern fringe of the Wall Street district, in Ann, Nassau, and Barclay Streets. Andrews could find respite from the stink of the leather and hide district east of City Hall with a short walk downtown, Chew with a short walk uptown from No. 49 Wall Street. Today the area is a morass of opticians and shoe shops with only the Isaac Mendoza Book Company, founded in 1894, surviving in Ann Street to solace the bibliophile on jury duty. Isaac Mendoza's last son died in 1972.

By 1900 several booksellers were established in the Astor Place area, that is, Eighth Street and Fourth Avenue. That was the origin of what remains the out-of-print center in New York. Today the rare book dealers can be found anywhere but south of Fortieth Street.

In the library of the Grolier Club I have examined the runs of New York bookseller catalogs of the late nineteenth century. Many of the dealers handled very important books indeed and obviously traveled frequently to replenish their stocks. Even Joseph Sabin dealt in the best-known English authors of the sixteenth and seventeenth centuries. Several dealt regularly in "illuminated missals" though it is difficult to judge their quality from the reverent descriptions.

It may come as a surprise to some that Beverly Chew's first affection in collecting was for American writers, especially Lowell, Longfellow, and Whittier. Upon arriving in New York in 1872, he began to collect these and others at an average price for first editions of fifty cents or a dollar. The trade in them was informal and bibliography as we know it was nonexistent. For years booksellers' lists—and lists they were, not catalogs—constituted "bibliography." Chew himself wrote (anonymously) the first bibliography of Longfellow, published in 250 copies by W. E. Benjamin, the bookseller, in 1885.

That was the year that Leon & Brother, booksellers at Fifth Avenue and Twenty-third Street, issued the landmark *Catalogue of American Authors.* It makes clear that while the fifty cents days were over, the one to ten dollar days had just arrived. The most expensive author in the Leon catalogue is Longfellow and his most expensive book, the *Poems on Slavery* (1842) at $40, is followed by his *Outre Mer* (1833) for $35 and *Evangeline* (1847) at $25. Hawthorne and Benjamin Franklin also ran extremely well. Lowell and Emerson run one dollar through ten dollars. Poe is in with the 1831 *Poems* and the 1840 *Tales* each at $25.

Tamerlane and *Al Aaraf* are listed but unpriced. Poor Melville is included, four novels but not *Moby Dick,* each at $1.50. Rather surprisingly he ranks exactly with the novels of Henry James, also $1.50 each.

William Evarts Benjamin, who founded his firm in 1884, issued a similar catalog in 1893 but with some pretty steep price increases. Poe's 1831 *Poems* is in for $250. What copy could this have been? Benjamin also announced a Print Department—"50,000 prints suitable for extra-illustrating," a disease which Andrews contracted with terrible virulence.

All this activity from at least 1872 onward ended in the unexplained decision by Chew in 1900 to sell his American collection to Jacob Chester Chamberlain, the gifted and enigmatic electrical engineer who died in 1905 at age forty-five. In 1909 Chamberlain's fine library was sold at an historic auction and dispersed forever. Chamberlain had set new, high standards in American collecting and bibliography. His Grolier Club catalog of Hawthorne was the standard bibliographical reference for years. Surely Chew recognized a kindred spirit when he relinquished his books to Chamberlain.

Chew simultaneously collected Early American leather bindings to 1850, a genuine pioneer undertaking virtually unacknowledged until the recent Michael Papantonio catalog and the work of William Spawn belatedly gave him due credit. The important Grolier Club catalog of Early American bindings of 1907, almost certainly all belonging to Chew, remains without ownership attribution in most card catalogs today. The fascinating and rare invoices from Valentine Nutter, an eighteenth-century New York binder, Nos. 124 and 125 in the 1907 Grolier catalog and now in the Club's library, must have been Chew's gift.

Yet another aspect of Chew's American interest was his collection of Early American bookplates, now also at the Grolier Club, given apparently upon his retirement in 1920–21.

In passing I mentioned Andrews's penchant for "Grangerizing" or extra-illustration. This was a common pastime among nineteenth-century collectors on both sides of the Atlantic and Andrews was a busy practitioner. Daniel M. Tredwell's out-of-the-way monograph *On Privately Illustrated Books* (1892) states specifically that the art of Grangerizing took firm hold in the United States around 1875 and cites dozens of collectors and their prizes. Andrews comes in for high praise from Tredwell: "Their intrinsic value consists in being the depositories of historical matter in manuscripts, autographs, portraits, and prints. In many respects it is the rarest collection in the city; much of it is now absolutely unique. Mr. Andrews was a disciple of John Allan, from whom he received his first inspiration in book-illustrating."[2]

How Andrews found the extra time for all this extra-illustrating baffles us today. Set after set of historical and literary works were taken apart, prints and autographs selected and inlaid, and then sent to the best New York binders of the time to emerge four or six times the length of the original work on the shelf. Let Andrews himself speak on the subject in a 1908 apologia and then we may let the subject rest:

> I must confess to long years of indulgence in the severely criticised but fascinating and at one time highly popular practice of "Extra Illustration" . . . If the book to be 'extra illustrated' is well chosen and taste and discrimination are exercised in its embellishments, the outcome will be as satisfactory in this as in many other lines of book-collecting. Only the ultra-refined bibliophile will deny that a Pepys's *Diary* interleaved with the quaintly beautiful "graven effigies" of the XVII century . . . are interesting and desirable additions to a collection of fine books . . . When it comes to crowding a Bible or a Shakespeare with engravings by the thousand in sets of dreary uniformity as long as your arm, we confess that "extra illustration" is a delusion and a snare and a weariness to the flesh.[3]

Not so weary, however, to preclude a prediction of a Second Coming:

> In the last ten years or a dozen years Grangerism has lost much of its former vogue, but I am under the impression that like fashions in dress there will be a revival of it, at least in a modified form.[4]

The fastidious Beverly Chew was moved to poetry on the subject, ending his amusing "On an Extra-Illustrated Copy of *Nell Gwynn*" with these final words:

> . . . ah, ruthless wight,
> Think of the books you've turned to waste
> With patient skill![5]

The privately printed books of William Loring Andrews were one of

---

2. Daniel M. Tredwell, *A Monograph on Privately Illustrated Books: A Plea for Bibliomania* (Flatbush, New York: Privately Printed, 1892), p. 252.

3. William Loring Andrews, *Bibliography of Books Issued in Limited Editions by William Loring Andrews During the Years 1885 to 1908 Inclusive* (Yearbook of The Grolier Club of New York for 1921), p. 142.

4. Ibid., p. 143.

5. William Bradford Osgood Field, ed., *Essays & Verses About Books by Beverly Chew* (n. p.: Privately Printed, 1926), p. 15.

his primary preoccupations and the means by which his name, through the booksellers' and auction catalogs, has remained prominent.

Between 1865–67, Andrews issued four items. Two were by his friend FitzGreene Halleck and were issued by subscription; the two others were kept for presentation. Between 1885, the Aldine catalog, and 1908, *The Heavenly Jerusalem,* Andrews wrote and saw through the press no less than twenty-six books, better than one a year. They dealt with bibliophilic and historical subjects dear to his heart and employed an enthusiastic style of writing not uncommon in the period. By far the larger number deals with New York history or early American engraving, constituting a serious contribution because Andrews owned all the original materials under discussion and consequently could use them as illustrations. Moreover, he often designed the title pages and end pieces himself, having a gentlemanly gift for drawing and watercolors. Some of these original designs survive in the scrapbooks and in Grolier Club special copies.

After examining each of these *bijoux* recently, I am bound to say I have a whole new respect for them. They are the precious self-indulgence of an affluent amateur but as books they are of very high quality. Andrews caught the gospel of acid-free and used only creamy Japan or fine handmade rag papers. The color illustrations, mostly by the Bierstadt gelatine process, are among the best color printing done in the United States during the period. One of Andrews's chief goals with his books was to preserve and encourage the art of copperplate engraving as an illustration process and so the exquisite engravings of Edwin Davis French and Sidney L. Smith figure in several. So strongly did Andrews feel on the subject of photographic illustration that he once wrote:

> It was an effort to show that it was still possible to dispense with these mechanical inventions in the making of a book, for highly developed as are the best of them, the trail of the camera, their progenitor, is over them all, and no picture that the photographer has had a hand in creating can ever be truly artistic or satisfying to an aesthetic sense.[6]

From evidence in the scrapbooks we know that up to 1895 the DeVinne Press did Andrews's printing but after that Gilliss Brothers did it all. Walter Gilliss says in his interesting *Recollections* (1926) that a happy collaboration on a Grolier Club project induced Andrews to switch from DeVinne to Gilliss. Maybe so, but it must have caused waves in that small pond. Trouble ahead can be seen in a letter from F. E. Hopkins, manager at DeVinne's and later himself proprietor of The Marion

6. Andrews, *Bibliography,* p. 144.

Press in Jamaica, New York. It shows a side of Andrews which poor Mr. Hopkins probably had to deal with often.

3 March 1894

Dear Mr. Andrews:

I sometimes think I will never give another estimate. It is only a guess, made before the work is actually done; and one cannot *help* omitting some items which he should have put in . . ." [here follows his troubles with the presswork, with printed captions, and with Andrews adding illustrations in mid-stream, and continues:] "When the work is finally done I will charge it just as low as possible; and you may congratulate yourself on having a Grolier book at *half-price*. Certainly the Club does not get its books for so little money as you get yours.

Very truly,

F. E. Hopkins

Little wonder that in 1895 Andrews took his custom to Gilliss Brothers.

Prior to 1896 I am uncertain how Andrews distributed copies of his books for sale but assume small quantities were taken by quality booksellers. After 1896 he made complicated copublication arrangements with Dodd, Mead & Co. and Charles Scribners' Sons. In London, the Andrews books were handled on a regular basis by Quaritch, which gave their begetter considerable satisfaction.

The scrapbooks make it perfectly clear that Andrews, an old New York merchant, kept a close eye on the sale of his books. Some of course, were presentations and the scrapbooks duly preserve processions of thank-you letters in which a trace of weariness can be detected, especially from, of all people, Beverly Chew and Samuel Putnam Avery. What did Chew really think when he, with the greatest reluctance in the world, pointed out to Andrews that a "printer's error" had inadvertently subverted Vergil and placed the poet *Ossian* on top of mount Pelion? Outside of his field of New York history, Andrews's scholarship was rambunctious and shaky, liberally sprinkled with foreign phrases and quotation marks.

Andrews's books were never cheap. The Japan edition of *Gossip About Book Collecting* (1900) was $34; *Bibliopegy in the United States* (1902) was $40. Frequently they sold out right away and began to rise in the rare book market and at auction. The newspapers in those days regularly reported auction results and invariably the Andrews books came first, as Major Abbey does today. In 1901, one New York newspaper made the astonishing remark that the only parallel to the rise in value of Mr. Andrews's books was that of the books of the Kelmscott

Press. Another said: "There is probably no American author whose books increase in value in anything like the proportion attained by those brought out by Mr. Andrews." At the Borden sale in 1913 (duly recorded in the scrapbooks) Andrews's privately printed books reached an average of $75 each, with one fantastic high of *Among My Books* (1894), which was never published for sale, of $420—printed on vellum and bound at The Club Bindery. The most recent prices for the books recorded by *American Book Prices Current* for 1970–75 range up to $225.

To conclude this section on Andrews are words he said himself:

> The construction of these books has involved numerous experiments in present day book-making more or less costly, both in time and money. Few of them have been completed in less than a year. The final act in the case of each one was the consignment to the waste basket of a quantity of rejected sheets. Frequently we would find ourselves in possession of perfect copies considerably in excess of the number called for in the certificate of the book, and these we were necessarily obliged puncti- liously to destroy. It seemed a wicked waste of paper, printer's ink and skilled labor, but it was unavoidable. In the effort to construct a good book one must not stop to count the cost in either money, time or pains.[7]

A study of the books produced by Andrews confirms his words. All things considered, they are a unique achievement.

Yet another activity dear to Andrews's heart was the founding and nurturing of the Society of Iconophiles in 1895, a worthy undertaking now largely forgotten. As Andrews said, they were ". . . a few kindred spirits, lovers of Old New York, imbued with a feeling of civic pride in its past and present . . ." that in spite of its Greek name was really "a Society for the Propagation of Pictures of the City of New York, Ancient and Modern." Their purpose was to issue reproductions of his- toric views of the city and to commission living artists (of an assuredly conservative stripe) to record the present-day city. The contemporary artists commissioned were to work only in engraving or lithograph. The quality of the 119 prints thus issued was of the highest and they have been known in recent years to have changed hands as originals of the eighteenth or nineteenth century. For the deluxe copies of Iconophile publications in a requisite orange morocco whole herds of innocent goats died. The original membership was an inner ring of ten Grolier Club mem- bers, with fifty Associates expected to buy everything issued. The roster of Associates, of course, rings with the family names of old New York.

7. Andrews, *Bibliography,* p. 145.

The Iconophiles had their ups and downs, especially after the death of Andrews in 1920, and by 1930 called the whole thing off, issuing that year a large quarto history and bibliography. The remainder stock of books and prints, minute and account books, and correspondence were then given to the library of the Grolier Club.

Before returning to Andrews the book collector and the subsequent history of his library, a word should be said about his other collecting activities. Oriental porcelain—a typical nineteenth-century gentleman's hobby—took some of his attention. As early as 1883 Andrews gave the Metropolitan Museum (which he served as Trustee and Honorary Librarian for many years) ninety-two etchings by Haden and Whistler. Perhaps most interesting of all is the fact that he was one of only five New Yorkers to buy a painting from Durand-Ruel's first American exhibition of French Impressionists in 1886.

A library for Andrews was not a static affair and all through his adult life he was constantly buying and selling books. Doubtless because his son had died while a senior at Yale in the early 1880s and in thanks for an honorary degree conferred in 1893, Andrews in 1894 gave that library thirty-six early printed books illustrative of the first century of printing. Thirteen of these books came from the library of Michael Wodhull, ten came from Syston Park, and no less than seven had bindings by his particular hero, Roger Payne. These were eventually described in a catalog published by Yale in 1913.[8]

In November 1919 Andrews decided to sell his collections to the bookseller James F. Drake, reputedly for approximately a quarter of a million dollars. The scrapbooks and notebooks give no clue to this transaction but it cannot be questioned too deeply as Andrews lived for only five more months. Drake doubtless placed some items in good homes and then began to sell the remainder in a series of catalogs. No rhyme nor reason can be observed in this series except for the outstanding quality of each item, whether incunable, illustrated book, or binding. In short, the results of Andrews's collecting career, including the Americana, went through Drake's hands.

Drake originally planned to sell the Americana in a major catalog but decided in the press of business to send it to the Anderson Galleries for sale at auction in April 1921. It brought a total of $20,323.75 for 441 lots, a very disappointing total.

8. *Catalogue of the William Loring Andrews Collection of Early Books in the Yale University Library* (New Haven & London: Yale University Press & Oxford University Press, 1913).

The story does not quite end there. When Mrs. Andrews died in 1930, the Grolier Club learned it had inherited several choice items from her husband's collection. The bequest included a late eighteenth-century Dutch tall case clock, the Nathaniel Rogers miniature of FitzGreene Halleck given to Andrews by Halleck, three seventeenth-century Dutch silver bindings, a superb red morocco gilt binding by Roger Payne (ex-William Beckford), and another book, ex-T. F. Dibdin and William Beckford. The most unusual item in the bequest was the miniature Office of the Virgin printed on vellum by Jenson, Venice, 1475. As Goff 0-32 it remains the only copy known in America. We know that Andrews paid an English bookseller £42 for it in the late nineteenth century. Mrs. Andrews also included her husband's gold and amber cigar holder (which I have always held to be the perogative of the Grolier librarian to use).

We resume with Beverly Chew having sold his American collection to Chamberlain in 1900. But concurrently with his American collecting, Chew was also gathering a refined group of pre-1800 English writers' works which was the despair of his contemporaries. At some point this collection attracted the attention of Henry E. Huntington. The railroad mogul engaged George D. Smith, in continuum of their considerable business together, to begin to wear down Chew with the hope of acquiring his books. After several polite rebuffs, Chew inexplicably gave in sometime in late 1912, telling Edward G. Kennedy, "I really didn't want to sell, so mentioned a price that I doubted if anyone would pay." Indeed, the only record of a transaction is a receipt signed by Chew in the amount of $230,000. In this seemingly casual way, approximately 2,200 of the most carefully chosen English books in America changed hands.

The only reason for Chew's decision seems to be that the phenomenal prices brought in the Hoe sales of 1911–12 convinced him that the era of the collector with *relatively* modest means was over. Though a prosperous banker with no family commitments, Chew could not now possibly compete in the "age" of Morgan and Huntington.

But Chew exemplified the old rule of once a collector, always a collector, and book collecting was the main theme of his life. Two weeks after his books were sold, Chew began collecting again by buying the 1649 *Lucasta* at the Hoe sale. He now narrowed his focus even more— English poets of the Jacobean and Caroline periods, to be sure, but only the finest and most interesting copies. There were exalted writers and titles among them—Shakespeare, Milton, Dryden, and Pope—but primarily it was a collection of less well-known writers such as Richard Brathwaite, Abraham Cowley, Richard Crashaw, John Donne, George Herbert, James Shirley, and so on. There were also manuscript and printed "missals." Chew was a devout Episcopalian and in New York an active parishioner at St. Mary the Virgin, around the corner in 46th Street from his residence at the Royalton Hotel in West 44th Street. Though he was never known to discuss religion, I take his interest in prayer books, and the English prayer book in particular, to be a reflection of his lifelong interest in the higher reaches of Anglicanism.

So miscellaneous had been Henry E. Huntington's collection that the decision was made to disgorge duplicates. Between March 1916 and January 1924 no less than seventeen sales included Huntington duplicates. Chew seized this opportunity with delight, with the result that by the time of his death over 15 percent of his collection consisted of the very copies sold to Huntington in 1912! Robert H. Taylor wrote in 1967 that a "bibliophile may count himself lucky who is able to secure a Chew-Huntington-Chew book."[9]

Upon Chew's death in May 1924, the bibliophilic world learned that his library was to be removed from Geneva, New York, and sent to Anderson's for sale in December. This shows exceptionally brisk action for an executor but it helps when your family owns the local bank. In the first sale, 474 lots were sold; from the *Academy of Compliments* to Sir Henry Wotton. In January 1925 the post-1800 books and the bibliography were sold. Chew's favorite modern writers seem to have been Robert Bridges, Lewis Carroll, Austin Dobson, H. Rider Haggard, Rudyard Kipling, Frederick Locker, and Robert Louis Stevenson. It is interesting that Chew owned eleven Kelmscott Press imprints (but no Chaucer) and a collection of twenty-five first editions of the works of William Morris. The books in the two sales brought $159,228—unquestionably far more than they could have cost Chew. His print collection—not even mentioned here, for he loved portraits of English writers and certain Old Masters—was also sold.

Chew's "second" library was cataloged by the redoubtable Henrietta Bartlett, a close associate and his informal librarian for many years. She also wrote the introduction to the auction sale catalog. After the catalog cards were used to prepare the sale, they were presented by Chew's

9. *Grolier 75. A Bibliographical Retrospective to Celebrate the Seventy-Fifth Anniversary of The Grolier Club In New York* (New York: The Grolier Club, 1959), p. 52.

brother to the library of the Grolier Club, the only such catalog in its collection.

Chew's generosity to the Grolier continued with several important bequests. Throughout his membership, he had been exceptionally generous with gifts of books and pictures. It was his fond hope that the Grolier would become a National Portrait Gallery for American authors but the idea found no support outside his own enthusiasm and never came to anything. Apart from many interesting and useful books, in his lifetime Chew gave the Francis Lathrop grisaille oil portrait of James Russell Lowell in old age, and a particularly hair-raising gift—four folio scrapbooks (from the Hoe collection) of English and Continental title-leaves of the sixteenth and seventeenth centuries.

The Chew bequest included fifty-one bindings in silver, embroidery, and tortoiseshell, a class of books for which he had a particular affection. It seems that the silver bindings—mostly German of the eighteenth-century—represent an Achilles heel in Chew's collecting taste because they do not bear comparison with the best examples of the type. My guess is that since he did not travel among the European booksellers, he simply bought what came his way in New York.

Another part of the bequest included four portraits which hang today in the Club. Purchased in the era of optimistic attribution, only two of the four retain their original identity. The fine profile of Alexander Pope is at least from the workshop of Sir Godfrey Kneller and the Ben Jonson is a contemporary copy of the Honthorst in London. But the pastel portrait by Edward Luttrell, né Dryden, has turned into Thomas Otway and the so-called Dryden by Kneller is now a portrait by the interesting Restoration female artist Mary Beale of her n'er-do-well book-collecting husband, Charles.

Unlike the death of William Loring Andrews, a by-passed figure from horse-and-buggy New York, Beverly Chew's death brought out affectionate and unequalled tributes from the bibliophilic world. There were thirteen newspaper obituaries of him, all attesting to his virtues as a man, his knowledge as a scholar, and his judgment and skill as a collector. It is impossible to quote from them but they may all be seen in the splendid series of scrapbooks kept by the Grolier librarian, Ruth S. Granniss, for nearly fifty years. She had a particularly close and affectionate association with Chew and even attended his funeral in Geneva.

Chew was given the unusual tribute of a special Grolier meeting and the remarks were printed in the *Gazette*. Among the numerous recollections full of affection and admiration, one stands out in which the writer says that, after knowing Chew for many years, he found it impossible to crystalize his personality in words. Still, his character as man and collector was such that all who knew him considered him the living embodiment of the ideals and purposes of the Grolier Club.

Chew worked hard for the Grolier, serving on all committees and taking a particularly active part in exhibitions and publications. When he tackled a major exhibition, such as the Milton commemoration of 1909, the work was thorough to the highest degree. His attention to detail, seen in innumerable lists, memoranda, and letters, all in the midst of a busy banker's life, is remarkable. Perhaps one of the most interesting and significant of his contributions was the conception and supervision of the Grolier edition of the poetry of John Donne of 1895, the first modern edition, based on work begun by James Russell Lowell and carried to completion by Charles Eliot Norton. It was a project dear to Chew's heart. He was also the moving force behind the Club's publication *One Hundred Books Famous in English Literature* (1902) and the three-volume *Wither to Prior* (1905). He amazed his subalterns by correcting proof without recourse to reference books. Indeed, he was known to correct reference books, such as they were in those days.

In contrast to Andrews's harmless prolixity, Chew's bibliography is scanty. Miss Granniss wrote just after his death:

> As a writer, Mr. Chew is less known. His ventures into authorship were infrequent and very modest; but for clarity, concise description, and keen appreciation of the points, literary and bibliographical, of books for which he cared, his occasional writings are so noteworthy that keen regret has often been expressed that they are so few and so comparatively inaccessible.[10]

This inaccessibility was cured temporarily by the publication, just after Chew's death, of fourteen pieces in a volume sponsored by William Bradford Osgood Field, president of the Grolier Club, called *Essays and Verses About Books*. Printed in 275 copies by D. B. Updike, it is itself today quite a scarce book. The small collection includes poetry and short pieces on American catalogs, engraving, Waller, Milton, and the introductions to the Hoe and Hagan catalogs. Excluded are the Longfellow reference book, family pieces, and the traditionally anonymous contributions to Grolier Club catalogs. During his lifetime, Chew's most restricted effort was a short poem called "On a Leaf from a Fourteenth

---

10. Field, *Essays and Verses,* p. v.

Century Missal" printed on vellum in 1901 by the Gilliss Brothers in an edition of three. In this one instance he outdid Andrews.

Mentioned much earlier was the collection of letters to Chew from his friends, presented to the Grolier by his brother. It is sadly typical that we should have this representation of letters to him and, apart from working files in the Grolier archives, nothing from him. From among this trove, a few excerpts are quoted here to give the flavor of the times and Chew's friendships.

A small group from Harry Elkins Widener confirms all the fine things said about him since his death on the Titanic and further confirms Chew's position as elder statesman, father-confessor, and friend. Widener wrote on December 13, 1909:

> My dear Mr. Chew—
>   I am working on a catalogue of a few of my more important books and take the liberty of asking you one or two questions . . . Dr. Rosenbach has offered to do [the collations] for me and I should like to have him do it if in your opinion he is competant. Of this I am sure the Doctor will do his best and I am afraid if anyone else helped it might hurt his feelings, a thing I would not like to do . . .

Widener wrote again on October 1, 1911:

> Dear Mr. Chew;
>   This is just a few lines to tell you I am home again and to know how soon you can get out here to see us. I had a glorious time abroad, indeed the best time I have ever had. I met Mr. Wise who gave me a glorious time and showed me some wonderful books . . . As for books the very fine things were few and high. I got several books I want you to see . . .

Charles Eliot Norton wrote from Shady Hill, Cambridge, January 16, 1895, deep in the midst of the Grolier Club John Donne project, to thank Chew for the gift of the Club's *Transactions II,* just completed by Gilliss Brothers:

> . . . Most of Mr. William Morris's books, with *some* excellent qualities, seem to me to show lamentable want of perception of what makes a book really a notable monument of a fine art . . .

You will recall that Chew eventually owned eleven Kelmscott Press books and twenty-five Morris first editions—the only modern press in which he showed any interest at all.

Theodore Low DeVinne, born in 1828, dean of American printers and a founder of the Grolier Club, wrote within six years of his death on November 3, 1908:

My dear Mr. Chew:

   I have a high regard for Poe, but I think the proposed memorial of him by the Grolier Club should have been undertaken earlier . . . I am confirmed in this opinion by the negative votes that Poe has received for admission to the Hall of Fame of this city. It is certain that there have been and there are objections to the *man* if not to his writings.

Despite this prejudice, the Club issued a bronze medallion of Poe in 1909.

   Samuel Putnam Avery and Robert Hoe enjoyed close friendships with Chew, Hoe often writing as son would write to a father, though Hoe was eleven years older. Here is a pertinent excerpt, Avery to Chew, in August 1897:

   Quaritch writes that our friend R. H. has bought some things from him —but has not given permission to tell what. I hope he will bring home *the* Bible and other gems. With his means, youth, and love & knowledge one can hardly measure the complete greatness which his collection of books will attain to.

Hoe did indeed buy his Gutenberg Bible on vellum from Quaritch—for $25,000. At his sale it went to Huntington for $50,000, for many years a record for a printed book at auction.

   Hoe himself writes in a very long letter from the French town of Moulins in September 1890:

   One thing I do remember, and that is a large Ms. Bible I have just seen here in the library, in the old chisled bronze and enamel mountings on oak covers. These ornaments are intact, & the book itself on vellum with over 100 miniatures, all bright and dated 1015. It is the finest thing of the kind I ever saw. They got it out & let me turn it over as I liked: said the National Library of Paris had offered the town 150,000 francs & I thought it not worthwhile to bid higher . . .

This is a good example of the infectious enthusiasm which Hoe's contemporaries often remarked on.

   Hoe writes again, from London, July 1904:

   Day before yesterday I went down in the afternoon to Rowfant to see *Locker's* library. It is in the country, about 32 miles out, on the way to Brighton. The books are in a sort of oblong cell, with iron door and barred window, no light much. Most of the *rarest* volumes are in poor condition—imperfect & dirty. Young Locker thinks they are fine & am sorry not to agree with him.

Marshall C. Lefferts, New York grandee and book collector, was another close friend. This letter reflects the frequent contact among Lefferts, Chew, J. H. Wrenn of Chicago, and Thomas J. Wise:

> My Dear Chew
> Wrenn is "stung" again—he has written that he has received from Wise—who has had it bound by Riviere—a copy of Tate's "Character of Vertue and Vice—1691" and quotes from Wise "It is not included among the series of books by Tate described in the Hoe catalogue; it is not mentioned in the Grolier Club's "Poets Laureate" Bibliography and it is not to be found in any of the catalogues I possess—if this signifies that you possess the only copy owned in America I heartily congratulate you for the book holds an important place in literature, &c., &c.
> I have written Wrenn thanking him and Mr. Wise for having called my attention to it and enclosing a cutting from Pickering's last cat. offering a copy "sewn" @ £ 1.4. Cheap for such a unique book.

Finally, A. V. S. Anthony, New York surgeon, introduced to Chew by Edwin Clarence Stedman, wrote on November 28, 1896:

> My dear Mr. Chew:
> Our mutual friend, Mr. E. C. Stedman, tells me that you are a collector of literary bric-a-brac. I have all the letters of Mrs. Harriet Beecher Stowe concerning her book "The Vindication of Lady Byron," with several others on the same subject, about 45 in all. I have also the original draft of her letter to Prince Albret, to accompany a copy of "Uncle Tom's Cabin," which she sent to him.
> I have also all of Walt Whitman's letters in the matter of the publication, and suppression, of his "Leaves of Grass," with these in a volume in which Mr. Whitman marked, with his initial, the four passages which he would consent to change, and in the same volume are marked, by the District Attorney of Boston, the many passages which he indicated should be expunged in pain of supression. There is also a separate list of the objectionable lines, evidently made out by some vestal virgin in the attorney's office.
> I also have the ms. of Mark Twain's witty Montreal speech on copyright and literary matters, ending with some Ollendorf French.
> Do these items sound inviting to you? If so, I can send, or bring them to you, or they can be seen at my house. I am advised the lot is worth $200.

If asked what characterized book collecting in late nineteenth-century America, one would have to answer "opportunity." But the more things change, the more they are the same. Here is a passage so modern-sounding it could have been overheard at the Grolier Club any evening this year:

Sir:

The dealer who furnishes your interviewer with the remarkable statement as to the ease and cheapness with which he is able to secure rare
books, should congratulate himself on his good fortune . . . The melan-
choly truth is that the book-hunter's lot was never a harder one than it
is today. The process of absorption into public libraries, especially in this
country, has been going on for many years, and the limited supply virtually exhausted. The rarest of all things today is a rare book of value
and interest.

This was written by none other than William Loring Andrews to the
New York *Commercial Advertiser* newspaper for July 23, 1888.

Series design by Vladimir Reichl
Composed by FM Typesetters
in Times Roman Linotype
Printed on 50# Warren's Olde Style, a pH neutral stock,
by American Publishers Press and
Bound by Zonne Bookbinders